African Spiritual Practices

The Ultimate Guide to Yoruba, Santería, Orishas, Black Spirituality, Ancestral Veneration, Maat, Haitian Voodoo, and Hoodoo

Your Free Gift
(only available for a limited time)

Thanks for getting this book! If you want to learn more about various spirituality topics, then join Mari Silva's community and get a free guided meditation MP3 for awakening your third eye. This guided meditation mp3 is designed to open and strengthen ones third eye so you can experience a higher state of consciousness. Simply visit the link below the image to get started.

https://spiritualityspot.com/meditation

Table of Contents

Introduction

When people think of spirituality, their minds often turn to Asian and Western practices, such as Yoga, Wicca, Paganism, and Druidism. However, there are many more spiritual practices worldwide to learn about, and the African continent is home to several vibrant and fascinating spiritual traditions.

Some of the many spiritual traditions in Africa include Kemeticism (or Egyptian neo-paganism), Isese (or the Yoruba religion), Haitian Voodoo, Hoodoo, and Santeria. Most books on spiritual traditions only focus on well-known traditions, omitting these vibrant traditions altogether. In contrast, this book highlights these spiritual traditions and explores their associated practices extensively.

This book opens with an overview of the African spiritual practices that later chapters explore in further detail. We look at how each spiritual community is structured and how rituals are conducted. We look at some of their beliefs so readers can comprehensively understand each tradition.

Next, the book explores Ma'at, Kemeticism, and Kemetic Orthodoxy and looks at ways to invite Ma'at (cosmic order) into your life. It looks at the seven principles and 42 laws of Ma'at and explains how readers can include and follow them.

After exploring Ma'at, the book delves into the traditions of supreme creator gods in African spiritual traditions and how those following these practices believe the world was created. This chapter explains how these creator gods are worshipped.

The fourth chapter explores the Lwa and the Orishas – the gods and spirits of Haitian Voodoo and Isese. It will examine the pantheons of each spiritual tradition and help readers better understand how practitioners venerated and communicated with these deities.

Next, the book looks at the mysterious spiritual tradition of Santeria and the saints that are significantly important in this tradition. It explores the links between Santeria and Catholicism, Haitian Voodoo, and Isese and helps readers to understand how to invoke each saint's powers.

The sixth chapter expands on the African continent's strong tradition of ancestral veneration. Readers will better understand why ancestors are revered and how different spiritual traditions and religions practice ancestor veneration.

After exploring ancestor veneration, the book looks at some of Africa's sacred herbs and plants and their significance in rituals and spells in African spiritual traditions like Hoodoo. We also explore the roles of altars and shrines in these traditions and help you to understand how to build your altar for personal use.

Then, we cover in detail two common talismans in mojo bags and gris-gris. It teaches you how to create and use each of these talismans, providing a source of protection and magic wherever you go.

Finally, we examine the festivals and ceremonies celebrated in these African spiritual traditions. Since African traditions remain relatively unknown, there is a limited understanding of their religious celebrations, and this chapter seeks to remedy this concern.

This book also offers a glossary of terms, making it easier to understand the spiritual practices it covers. Since these practices are often accompanied by new and unknown terms, learning about them can be challenging.

So, without further ado, let's explore the world of African spiritual practices and uncover its many secrets.

Chapter 1: Getting to Know African Spiritual Practices

Many different unique cultural and spiritual practices stem from African and African American religions. From Senegal to South Africa, these practices are often connected with spirituality, ceremonies, rituals, and other traditions varying from one area to the next. Some are still practiced today, while others have been lost to time. These practices have been passed on from generation to generation and vary from tribe to tribe. Some were practiced by all community members, while others were reserved for specific people (often those having great power or potential). This chapter examines some of the most popular African spiritual practices and their history.

African spiritual practices span all over the African continent.
https://unsplash.com/photos/Ue5kuMVmIhU

Yoruba

The Yoruba people have a rich and complex history that is still studied by modern historians. The Yoruba religion is one of the largest African diaspora groups, with members spread across the globe. From recorded documents, the Yoruba people originated in West Africa, primarily Nigeria, Benin, and Ghana, where they lived peacefully and independently for many centuries. The Yoruba faith is one of the oldest religions in the world. Over 5000 years ago, the Yoruba people came into contact with European explorers, traders, and Muslim and Christian missionaries, who influenced their practices and beliefs. Several Yoruba groups converted to Christianity during this period, while others embraced Islam. Still, many maintained the traditional practices of their ancestors, resulting in a diverse and widely practiced religion that continues as an essential part of Yoruba culture. While there has been some variation in their beliefs over the centuries, the Yoruba religion is generally defined by a polytheistic belief system (multiple deities), a focus on ancestor worship, and a central role for divination, known as Ifa. Through this divination system, followers can understand the intent of the Supreme Being Olodumare.

During the slave trade, many Africans were forced to convert to Catholicism. However, Yoruba represented their history and identity. They couldn't simply abandon their roots. They practiced their faith secretly by merging some Yoruba aspects with Catholicism, blending many of the Orishas with Catholic saints. Holding on to their faith was a form of rebellion against enslavement and the loss of their freedom.

Beliefs of the Yoruba Religion

The Yoruba people believe that their supreme deity, Olodumare, created the universe. With help from lesser spirits, Olodumare formed the Earth and everything on it, including humans. People should strive to live according to Olodumare to be blessed with good fortune. According to the Yoruba religion, Ashe represents the energy found in all natural things, including humans and deities.

The Yoruba religion primarily focuses on worshipping deities called Orishas. These deities are often associated with natural forces like animals, plants, and the environment. They are good and bad spiritual beings (egungun and ajogun). Although they are not as powerful as Olodumare, the Orisha can perform important tasks, including healing and protecting humans from evil forces. In return for gifts and offerings, the Orisha protects the people and provides them with special gifts.

Yoruba Rituals and Customs

Yoruba rituals are sacred and secular, ranging from religious ceremonies to daily life. Traditional Yoruba rituals are done for many reasons, including celebrating a person's birth, marriage, or death. They also maintain harmony and balance in the community. The most critical aspect of Yoruba rituals is respect for all people. In Yoruba culture, everyone is equal. People have different roles and responsibilities within the community, but everyone has value and worth. Rituals show respect for those who have gone before by commemorating their lives and ensuring future generations are cared for in their absence. These ceremonies have immense meaning and vary significantly across the various West African communities.

One interesting aspect of the Yoruba religion is the relationship between priests and followers. While many religions have a strict hierarchy with a few individuals (e.g., priests, ministers, etc.) at the top, Yoruba priests are typically not seen as spiritually superior to the rest of the community. Instead, priests are seen as advisors, teachers, and healers who have studied and are knowledgeable in matters of the spirit. Priests are typically chosen by their communities to lead worship and perform essential ceremonies, but they do not hold a high spiritual authority position. Moreover, there is no central organization or hierarchical leadership within the Yoruba religion. Each community is autonomous and has the freedom to practice and interpret the religion as they see fit.

While most Yoruba religion practitioners belong to one of the many distinct lineages comprising the Yoruba community, every practitioner must adhere to some basic tenets. The first tenet is that one must be initiated into the religion as a child by a community member trained to perform this task. This initiation must take place between birth and adulthood, but it is most common for initiations to occur when children are between 5 and 7 years old. After being initiated into the religion, it is vital to learn what it means to be a Yoruba person. These principles include honoring your ancestors, respecting your elders, and observing traditional laws and customs.

They also include how to behave in public, such as in churches and markets, so as not to offend others or disgrace your family. However, above all else, not forgetting to live with purpose and meaning in your life is essential.

Santeria

While Yoruba is an ethnic group, Santeria is a religion developed by the Yoruba in Cuba and their descendants. Santeria is an Afro-Caribbean religion created by Atlantic slaves brought to Cuba, Puerto Rico, and other Caribbean islands between the 16th and 19th centuries. The enslaved people took many of their traditional African beliefs with them to the Caribbean, which were transformed over time into the Santeria religion. It is not just one religion but a synthesis of traditional Yoruba beliefs, Spiritualism, and Roman Catholic Christianity.

Beliefs of the Santeria Religion

There is no one set doctrine or dogma within Santeria. Instead, there are multiple sects with slightly different beliefs and practices. However, Santeria is polytheistic and revolves around the same multi-Orisha deities as the Yoruba people. It emphasizes the idea that all things have a spirit and that spirits come from the gods who created the universe. People who practice Santeria believe they can communicate with these spirits and ask them for help. The main goals of this religion are to honor and respect the spirits.

Santeria Rituals and Customs

In this religion, practitioners engage in rituals and ceremonies to connect with the spirit world. These rituals worship deities, and their ceremonies involve drumming, dancing, and chanting. They also include prayers, offerings, and fasting. These rituals are often guided by a santero (male) or santera (female). In addition to acting as a spiritual medium for its practitioners, Santeria allows followers to connect with their ancestors through rootwork and spirit possession rituals. Some practitioners believe they can communicate with their ancestors through these mediums.

The extent of participation in Santeria varies greatly. The practice of Santeria recognizes three primary deities, each with its associated ritual practices. The most important deity is the Orisha, which comes from the Yoruba people of West Africa. There are many Orisha, and some are honored in more than one form of Santeria.

The rituals of Santeria are divided into different categories reflecting the spirit being honored. Any ritual can be described as "Santeria" as long as it honors one or more deities. Each category has specific steps that must be followed to honor the particular spirit properly. For example, some ceremonies involve elaborate offerings and dances that allow participants to communicate with the honored spirit. Others focus mainly on spiritual cleansing and healing through prayer and herbs. Some ceremonies also involve animal sacrifice to appease the spirit being honored and bring protection.

Haitian Voodoo

During the Atlantic slave trade of the 16th to 19th centuries, Haitian Voodoo, also known as Vodou, developed among Afro-Haitian communities. Yoruba, Fon, and Kongo, among other enslaved West and Central Africans, came to Hispaniola with their traditional religions melded together. Over time, the religion evolved to include elements from indigenous religions and Christianity. It combines native spiritual beliefs and practices from Catholicism and is characterized by worshipping spirits and ancestors. Many people around the world currently practice voodoo. Globally, 60 million practitioners follow one of several variations of the faith. Some Haitian Voodoo practitioners trace their ancestry back to those brought to Haiti as enslaved people. Others claim direct descent from those born there or moved there after slavery was abolished. People of both backgrounds practice Voodoo, either out of belief or curiosity. The followers of Voodoo are referred to as Vodouisants.

In many ways, Haitian Vodou is similar to African religions. For example, Haitian Vodou rituals often involve foods, drinks, and herbs for healing and spiritual purposes. Like many other religions of the African diaspora, Haitian Vodou has been influenced by Christianity. Many Haitians are Christians who practice some elements of their ancestor's religion alongside their Christian beliefs.

Vodou is considered a syncretic religion because it incorporates elements from multiple sources. These sources include African religion and Christianity. One thing that sets Haitian Vodou apart from Yoruba and Santeria is their theology. In this theology, worshipping a single deity is combined with worshipping multiple deities (polytheistic).

There is a misconception that Voodoo is associated with dark magic, violence, and devil worship. However, this is an unfair representation of a peaceful religion with no relation to witchcraft. For centuries, Voodoo has suffered from many misunderstandings that led people to fear and to be curious about it. Hollywood didn't help by constantly portraying it as a method to cause people harm.

A famous incident in Haiti in 1791 could have sparked controversy and misunderstandings around Voodoo. There was a peaceful Voodoo ceremony many witnesses misinterpreted as participants making a deal with the devil. Violent slavery revolutions resulting afterward led white settlers to make these negative associations.

Voodoo dolls are also misrepresented in pop culture as tools to perform black magic and bring pain and suffering to others. Vodouisants assign specific dolls to their Lwa and use them to invoke assistance or guidance.

Beliefs of Haitian Voodoo

The religion can be challenging to define because it draws from many sources and contains many traditions. However, Voodoo is characterized by its emphasis on magic and ancestor worship. Some voodoo religions believe that spirits can possess people, animals, and objects (Loa). Others worship gods and goddesses. Also, different types of magic are part of Voodoo. Some magic rituals use animal sacrifices. Others use potions or powders believed to have special powers. Voodoo rituals often involve dancing, chanting, and drums. Offerings are sometimes made to gods and goddesses during these ceremonies.

Haitian Voodoo Rituals and Customs

Vodoun priests can be male or female. Male priests are called Oungan, while female priestesses are called Manbo. Both perform initiation rituals such as bowing, chanting, and praying in an effort to communicate with spirits or Iwa. They are responsible for administering blessings, charms, and rituals for sick people and curing illness through prayer. Besides possessing knowledge about voodoo rituals, mambos have expertise in herbal medicine, using herbs in their potions and for healing purposes.

Hoodoo

Voodoo and Hoodoo are often used interchangeably, but there is a difference.

Voodoo is a religion, while Hoodoo is not. In addition to rituals, teachers, and leaders, Voodoo has two distinct branches; New Orleans Vodou and Haitian Vodou. In contrast, Hoodoo is not a religion, has no organizational structure, and is performed by individuals claiming to possess certain magical powers, each with their distinctive style.

In Hoodoo, Christianity, Spiritualism, African religion, and Islam are combined into a syncretic spiritual system.

There are many misconceptions about Hoodoo - it is like Voodoo, or its practitioners are fortune-tellers. In reality, Hoodoo is a blend of various practices to interact with the spiritual world. It is a religion that evolved from the West African tribal religions brought to the Americas by enslaved Africans. Nowadays, it is often associated with the African-Americans culture in the South, Southwest, and Northeast United States.

Hoodoo is a southern U.S. form of magic originally brought over to the U.S. by enslaved Africans. It remained an important tradition in the southern U.S. and continues to be practiced today. The religion evolved from the West African tribal religions brought to the Americas by enslaved Africans. Although its exact roots are disputed, scholars agree that Hoodoo's development can be traced to the 19th century. Beginning in the Southern states where most Africans were kept as slaves, Hoodoo evolved from a secret (hidden from slave owners) system of spiritual practices, initially used for healing and protection, into a religion that also addressed daily life problems.

Beliefs of Hoodoo

Hoodoo is the synthesis of various African and New World folk practices and traditions. Hoodoo practitioners believe a number of mystical forces are at work in the world. These include potent entities, spirits, and supernatural forces. They also believe these forces can be harnessed and used to improve people's lives. Hoodoo practitioners use a range of techniques to connect with these forces. Some techniques include casting spells, making potions, and performing rituals. They also use charms and talismans. All these techniques aim to create a connection between the practitioner and the mystical force they are attempting to harness. Once this connection has been created, the practitioner can influence or control the supernatural force. Hoodoo practitioners believe that mystical forces can be manipulated by using certain objects. These objects include stones or bones from animals like dogs or cats because some hoodoo practitioners believe these animals have supernatural powers.

Hoodoo Rituals and Customs

Hoodoo religion is a spiritual practice focusing on using magic, witchcraft, and Botanics. There are many different hoodoo spiritualisms, but they all share common elements. These include a belief in the power of nature and an emphasis on offerings to deities and spirits. Many hoodoo religions incorporate elements from other religions, like Christianity or African tribal beliefs. No established rules or laws govern the hoodoo religion, making it difficult for outsiders to understand. However, there are some basic practices most people in the religion can agree on. For example, most practitioners agree that magic requires an element of chance and includes rituals like fortune-telling. They also agree that any worship must be accompanied by at least some form of sacrifice or offering. Some common hoodoo rituals harness spirits for various uses, use lucky charms called mojo bags or lucky pieces to bring good fortune, and perform spells to change a person's or situation's outcome, and hexes to call upon or expunge negative energy.

Hoodoo priests are known as rootworkers. Rootworkers use hoodoo practices to help people with their problems or issues in life. They are also referred to as conjure doctors or conjure masters. While these terms can be used interchangeably, rootworkers are distinct from conjure doctors, who are usually herbalists using folk remedies to heal ailments. Rootworkers focus on using folk magic and spiritual practices, like hexes or spells, to help people with their problems. The hoodoo tradition is passed down from teacher to student, and students often have to go through a rite of passage before they can begin their studies. In some cases, students might undergo an initiation or test before they can begin their studies and become fully-fledged hoodoo practitioners.

Kemetic Orthodoxy

Less of a religion and more of a theology dedicated to the exploration of truth and knowledge through worshipping deities, Kemetic Orthodoxy is a religion based on the ancient Egyptian religion and way of life. It has been adapted and changed to fit modern life and values. It is a syncretic approach combining Christianity and other world religion elements to create a new synthesis. The faith focuses on the spiritual power of ancient Kemetic elements, including Egyptian gods and goddesses, mythical beasts, plants and animals, and sacred places such as temples, cemeteries, and burial grounds. It draws on an eclectic mix of sources, including the ancient Kemetic religion, neo-paganism, animism, African traditional religions, and Western religious traditions like Christianity and Judaism. Many people practice aspects of Kemetic Orthodoxy without necessarily identifying with the entire religion. In particular, Kemetics practice ancestral spirituality alone or combined with other forms of spirituality. For example, some may practice Kemetic Orthodoxy while also practicing Wicca or neo-paganism. Others practice Kemetic Orthodoxy while also following a more traditional Christian or Jewish path.

Kemetic Orthodoxy originated in the United States and has experienced significant growth since its founding in the 1980s by Rev. Tamara L. Siuda. It is now practiced globally by individuals and groups.

Beliefs of Kemetic Orthodoxy

Practitioners, known as Shemsu, are guided through the faith by five basic tenets:

- Taking part in the community and respecting it
- The belief in Netjer (the Supreme Being)
- The veneration of Akhu (ancestors)
- Upholding the principles of ma'at (morality and ethics)
- An acknowledgment of Siuda (the founder of the faith) as the Nisut (leader)

While Kemetic Orthodoxy believes in one divine power (Netjer), it is also a polytheistic religion believing in multiple deities, similar to Yoruba and Santeria.

Kemetic Orthodoxy Rituals and Customs

The practice of the faith is divided into three categories:

- **Formal or state worship**: All members are observed by a chosen priest and perform prayers at sunrise to a chosen deity

- **Personal piety**: All members, priests, and higher clergy give praise and worship the deities in an established Senut (shrine)

- **Ancestral devotion** through offerings and prayer

These are five of the many different African religions and spiritual practices that have existed for centuries. The practices vary significantly from one region to another. Each is based on various deities and different rituals and practices for worship. They are all unique, and their histories and traditions are fascinating. They provide a fascinating look into the history of these African regions and the people who lived there for centuries.

These religions are more than traditional practices but represent the African identity and roots. Even though the Abrahamic religions found their way to Africa, many people still hold onto their ancestors' traditions.

Chapter 2: Maat: Bring Harmony and Balance to Your Life

Maat, an ancient Egyptian goddess or a concept? Maat was a goddess but represented something more. She symbolizes order and harmony. Every king's duty was to ensure that Maat or order was established to replace disorder (Isfet) and chaos. Maat represented various significant notions in ancient Egyptian cultures, like truth and justice. Yet, Maat was also a powerful and influential goddess, the daughter of the creator god and the god of the sun, Ra. When Ra was creating the universe, Maat was created out of him, meaning Maat has existed since the beginning of time and brought balance and harmony to a chaotic universe. For this reason, many treated Maat as a concept to live by rather than a deity.

Maat represented order and harmony.

She didn't have a story like the other goddess or a personality. She merely represented a few crucial ideas. If you become one with Maat and her principles, you'll lead a balanced life and be guaranteed a peaceful eternity in the afterlife. However, if you reject her laws and principles, you'll suffer severe consequences in the afterlife. In other words, Maat represented the ideal behavior and characteristics to abide by and on which all other deities agreed. Maat was the foundation on which Ra built his creation and represented the rules the ancient Egyptians were instructed to follow.

Maat means "*that which is true and straight*," which signifies everything she represented. She is depicted as a woman with wings carrying the key of life (the ankh). Maat was cherished among ancient Egyptian kings and people, and her followers called themselves "Beloved of Maat." In some legends, she was married to her brother Thoth, the God of wisdom.

Each person had the choice to lead an honorable and honest life and abide by Maat's principles, or they could ignore them and live by their own rules. In other words, everyone was responsible for their actions without any gods' interference. The gods were fair. They left each person to their own, but they should also be prepared to face the consequences in the afterlife and pay for their mistakes. However, the gods still hoped that people would care about one another as they cared for them and lived in harmony. Living in harmony with the gods meant abiding by Maat's principles.

The ancient Egyptians, similar to many other cultures at the time, believed in the afterlife. How they would spend their afterlife depended on the life they chose to lead. Every person underwent a trial and judgment, referred to as "The Weighing of the Hearts."

The Weighing of the Hearts

After death, the soul of the dead arrives at a place in the afterlife called "The Hall of Truth." Whether he was a king or a peasant, everyone had to be tried and face the gods' judgment. The gods who judged the souls were referred to as the council of Maat. During each trial, the soul of the dead stood in front of the judges while the human body remained in its grave. However, only the aspects of the human soul would make it to the Hall of Truth for the trial.

The ancient Egyptians believed nine parts made up each person's soul.

1. The Khat (the physical body).
2. The Ren (a person's secret name).
3. The Ka (a person's double form).
4. The Ab (the heart which drives the person to be good or bad).
5. The Ba (a part of the soul that took the shape of a bird with a human head and could travel between the heavens and earth).
6. The Akh (the immortal self).
7. The Sahu (an aspect of the Akh).
8. The Sechem (another aspect of the Akh).
9. The Shuyet (the shadow self).

These nine parts represented the human soul's aspects that existed on Earth. After death, the Akh and its two aspects, Shuyet and Sechem, would travel to the underworld and stand before the god of the underworld, Osiris, to await their judgment in front of forty-two judges. Some of the most insignificant gods and goddesses in Ancient Egypt were among these judges, like the Creator Ra, Horus the god of the sun, Nut the goddess of the sky, Geb the god of the earth, Hathor the goddess of love, Shu the goddess of peace, Nephthys the goddess of the dead, and her sister Isis, the goddess of life. The fourth aspect of the soul, the Ab (heart), was placed on a golden scale and weighed against a white feather. However, this was no ordinary white feather; it belonged to Maat and was referred to as the feather of truth.

Before the heart was placed on the scale, the immortal self (the Akh) had to first recite the "Negative Confession" or "The Declaration of Innocence," which was a list of forty-two sinful actions to confess they never did. The confessions were made to each of the judges. Negative confessions differed from one person to another. They were tailored for each person because people are different, and the temptations they faced and the sins they committed aren't the same. For instance, a sin like "I never ordered a kill" was appropriate for a blacksmith who would normally never be involved in ending someone's life. However, kings, soldiers, and judges had probably been in a situation where they had ordered someone's death. Therefore, this sin wouldn't be included in their confessions since, in this case, it was their job, not a sin. Also, committing all the sins presented to them had to be denied. If a warrior denied killing someone, they would be lying. Therefore, there wasn't a standard list for each person, but there were some common sins that no person should ever commit, like stealing or cursing the gods. Intentions were significant in these confessions. For instance, the confession, "I never made someone cry." No one would attest if this were true because it could never be known if their actions or words had brought someone to tears. Their confession here was based on their intention, meaning they never intended to make someone cry.

The sins represented everything that went against Maat's principles. The ones who lived by her rules were virtuous, and even the sins they committed didn't have ill intentions. The purpose of these confessions was to show that each person understood life should only be lived according to the gods' teachings, not the person's whims.

After a person listed their confessions, their heart was placed on the scale. Even if they lied during confessions, their hearts would never lie. If they pretended to be virtuous, the scale would expose them. The heart of a good person would be lighter than the feather of truth. In this case, Osiris would consult with Thoth and the forty-two judges to determine if the person was truly worthy and should be rewarded. The gods would evaluate how many sins a person had committed and decide if they were on the virtuous or sinner side. However, if the heart was heavier than Maat's feather, they would be denied an afterlife. Unlike other religions, the ancient Egyptians didn't have a concept of hell. The goddess Ammut would devour the heavy hearts, and the person would no longer exist. Maat was depicted on top of the golden scale during the trial. However, other drawings showed her by Osiris's side.

After judgment was passed, the light hearts were allowed passage to The Field of Reeds, the ancient Egyptians' equivalent to heaven. However, the journey wasn't easy. Evil forces like demons created chaos and traps to prevent the soul from reaching its final destination. Those who managed to arrive safely would be reunited with their departed loved ones and spend eternity in the enchanted realm of the Field of Reeds. Other myths don't include the demonic traps - the souls lead an easy journey through Lily Lake, where they face one last test before they reach the Field of Reeds.

Maat protected this realm and all its residences. If a person was lucky enough and had a pure heart, they would get the chance to see Maat. Her role wasn't only to weigh hearts, but she also supported the souls of the people in the Field of Reeds who abided by her rules.

Maat's Role in Kemeticism

In the myth of creation in Kemetism, before there was mankind or creation, chaos was the only thing existing. Ra emerged from the chaos to create the universe. She was created as a power against chaos. Maat's role in Kemetism was similar to her role in ancient Egyptian religion. She was the keeper of order, harmony, and truth and prevented chaos. She represented justice and truth. Hence, her feather determined the worthiness of a person's heart. The concept of Maat and everything she represented was hugely significant in Kemeticism. The worshipers performed specific rituals and prayers to honor the laws of Maat and help spread them among others.

When the upper and lower of ancient Egypt were united, the Kemetism followers became aware of the forty-two rules of Maat, which they applied in their daily lives and used in their negative confessions. The weighting of hearts also took place in their belief in the underworld or duat against Maat's feather of truth. If Maat found that the person had abided by her laws, they were granted eternity in the Field of Reeds, where they would meet Osiris, who guarded its gates.

A Light Heart in the Spiritual Journey

A light heart will grant you eternity in paradise or the Field of Reeds. It signifies that a person has led an honest life and is in harmony with the gods. A light heart is a pure and virtuous heart. A person must guarantee their heart is light before embarking on a spiritual journey. A spiritual journey involves self-discovery, asking questions, finding answers, finding your place in the universe, awakening your spirit, and experiencing a rebirth. During this journey, you become aware of who you are and whom you are supposed to be.

A light heart is necessary on this journey. Another version of yourself inside of you'll be awakened during your spiritual journey - one who is more positive, confident, and powerful. Becoming the best version of yourself requires a pure heart that can let go of anger, greed, lying, and other vices and embraces positivity and light. Whether you take a spiritual journey to discover yourself, find your place in the universe, grow, connect with a deity, or move on from an unfortunate past, your heart has to be free of everything that ever held you back. Most people are led by their hearts, and an impure heart will prevent you from achieving your journey's purpose.

You can have a pure heart by following Maats' laws. Although these rules are ancient, they are still relatable and can still be applied. Many things have changed through the centuries, except what defines a good person. These timeless laws and principles will help you walk a straight path. They purify your heart of hate, anger, greed, envy, and everything that can taint it. You have the power to lead an honest life, even if it seems hard at times.

In Kemetic belief, applying Maat's principles is necessary to live a balanced life and have a light and pure heart.

The Seven Principles and Forty-Two Laws of Maat

This chapter has mentioned the principles and laws of Maat a few times. Here, you'll discover these principles and the laws which can be applied in modern times.

1. Order

Maat is the opposite of chaos, so it makes sense for its first principle to be "order." The universe wasn't created randomly. There is a pattern behind everything in creation. Everything is in order - the night follows the day, the planets revolve around the sun, and the moon goes through different cycles. Even in the world of the deities, there is a hierarchy, and every god and goddess knows their place. The god of the underworld won't leave his position to rule the skies or vice versa. Maat was created to bring order to a once chaotic universe and maintain its balance. Order is life, so it's the main focus of Kemeticism. Without order, the universe would succumb to chaos and perish.

You can apply the concept of order in life by keeping your environment organized, clean, and clutter-free.

2. Balance

Finding the balance between opposites in life is necessary. You shouldn't indulge in or lead a life of excess. For instance, a life with all play and no work is a waste of time, and a life with all work and no play can be hard and boring. Find balance in everything in life so you can live in harmony. In other words, coexist with nature. Don't empty its resources and only take what you need. You don't want to deprive future generations of Mother Nature's resources.

3. Justice

Justice is the foundation of life and one of the most significant of Maat's principles. Like the gods don't differentiate between kings and peasants, people should also treat everyone equally. Applying justice is living by an ethical code where you put what is right above everything else. It represents equality where no one goes hungry, and every person is allowed their basic needs - food, water, medical care, and a home. Everyone should be treated with respect regardless of their social status. If justice is applied, there will be less killing, stealing, and cheating.

4. Truth

Truth is honesty, whether you are honest with yourself about who you truly are and what you need or honest with others by sticking to the truth and avoiding lies. Living your truth requires you to see yourself for who you truly are and be your most true and authentic self without lying or faking. Everything you think, say, or do should be truthful. It is a sign of respect when you honor yourself and others with the truth.

5. Reciprocity

Reciprocity resembles the concept of karma or what goes around comes around. This concept is in many religions, like Christianity and Buddhism. If you do good deeds and treat everyone with kindness and respect, others will treat you in the same way, and good things will happen to you. However, bad deeds and disrespect will only bring negativity into your life.

6. Harmony

Harmony is achieved when people, plants, and animals live authentically and move together in alignment.

7. Propriety

Propriety is the understanding that all living creatures have the right to exist. All creatures, like animals, should also be left to live in peace without feeling threatened or harmed. It is similar to the ethical code behind vegetarianism and veganism. Propriety also implies that you shouldn't harm yourself or others with words or actions.

The Forty-Two Laws of Maat

The forty-two laws of Maat were derived from her seven principles.

1. I have never cursed.
2. I have never sinned.
3. I have never eaten more than I should.
4. I have never stolen.
5. I have never lied.
6. I have never killed.
7. I have never stolen from a deity.
8. I have never deceived the gods and goddesses with offerings.
9. I have never used violence to commit robbery.
10. I have never stolen food.
11. I have never been angry for no reason.
12. I have never ignored the truth.
13. I have never accused an innocent person.
14. I have never been unfaithful.
15. I have never eavesdropped.
16. I have never made someone cry.
17. I have never deceived anyone.
18. I have never felt sad for no reason.
19. I have never stolen someone's land.
20. I have never attacked anyone.
21. I have never violated my boundaries.
22. I have never seduced another man's wife.
23. I have never been reckless or acted without thinking.
24. I have never polluted myself.

25. I have never disrupted someone's peace.

26. I have never frightened anyone.

27. I have never been violent.

28. I have never broken the law.

29. I have never cursed a deity.

30. I have never been extremely angry.

31. I have never destroyed a temple.

32. I have never exaggerated the truth.

33. I have never been arrogant.

34. I have never committed evil.

35. I have never stolen food from a child.

36. I have never polluted water.

37. I have never disrespected the dead or stolen from them.

38. I have never spoken with arrogance or anger.

39. I have never stolen anything that belonged to a deity.

40. I have never cursed in deeds, words, or thoughts.

41. I have never put myself on a pedestal.

42. I have never used evil deeds, words, or thoughts.

You may feel guilty or discouraged that you have only just learned about these laws. However, it is never too late to start working on yourself. It doesn't matter what you did yesterday or who you were before. Now that you have learned about Maat's laws, you can start a new chapter in your life by following her rules. The rest of your life can start today.

Maat's laws will push you to be a better person, make you feel good about yourself and your life, and strengthen your relationship with others. If you aren't sure whether you need these rules or not, ask yourself:

- Am I happy with my life right now?
- Am I the best version of myself?
- Am I leading a life I should be proud of?
- Am I living an honest and authentic life?
- If I died today, would my heart be light or heavy?

- What can I do to be better and do better?

It will take time to memorize these laws to include them in your life. Help yourself by writing them in a note on your phone and reading them every day before you go to bed, and when you wake up, so they are always on your mind. You can write them as questions in your diary, like, have I lied today? Have I made someone cry? Was I arrogant? Was I angry for no reason? Or you could write each law on a small piece of paper, fold them, and put them in a bowl. Every morning randomly pick a piece of paper and do two or three things to apply the law.

Maat, as a concept or goddess, is a fascinating part of ancient Egyptian history. Everything she represented and her laws and principles can still be applied in the modern age. It will take time and effort to get accustomed to her teachings, but with persistence, you could have a light heart. Remember, having a light heart doesn't mean being perfect or committing no sins. It's about letting the good in you outweigh the bad.

Chapter 3: Supreme Creator Gods

In the belief systems of African cultures, supreme creator gods were responsible for creating people and the world. These are the most important and highest gods in the pantheon and have many commonalities. These gods have so much in common because they are likely derived from the same source. The similarities are further proof that an earlier pan-African religion fragmented over time and place as people settled, farmed, and adopted new practices. In addition to being creators, these supreme creator gods also are notably important in these cultures. For example, some are known as intermediaries between humans and other divine beings. Other supreme creator gods are less important but still have specific characteristics that make them stand out from the rest. This chapter explores the supreme creator gods in African-derived religions. For example, Yoruba religions worship Olodumare as their supreme being. Olodumare created and ruled all things. He determined the fate of humans and their characters. Bondye, another supreme being, is worshipped as the world's creator and sustainer of balance in Vodun.

The supreme creator gods are the highest order of deities.

Olodumare

Olodumare, also called Olorun or Olafin-Orunis, is the supreme deity venerated in the Yoruba religion, Santeria, Umbanda, Folk Catholicism, and Candomble. The word "olodumare" is a combination of two words: "olofin" and "odumare," meaning "noble spirit" and "lord." He is the god of creation and the master of all things. In short, he's the one who made everything possible. Olodumare is neither male nor female and is often called "they." Few people know about Olodumare. But for those who do, there may be more questions than answers. Who is this god, exactly? Why should we worship him? Why would anyone want to follow him?

Who is Olodumare?

Olodumare is the supreme deity in Yoruba religious traditions. As the creator and ruler of the universe, he is the ultimate source of all power. Olodumare is usually considered a monotheistic deity. His name means *"the owner of the house," "the owner of the market,"* or *"the king of the market."* In this case, the market is the world, and he is the owner. As the supreme deity and creator of all things in the Yoruba pantheon of gods and goddesses, he lives in the sky, where gods live. All creatures and spirits of the land, air, and sea are subject to him, but he is not omnipresent and does not walk on Earth, although he does remain active and responds to prayer.

Since the Yoruba religion is passed down orally, various versions of the same myths and legends exist. Some stories describe Olodumare as an absent deity who isn't involved in the lives of mankind. They live in Heaven, far away from the people and their affairs, and cannot even hear their prayers. Therefore, they created the Orishas as intermediaries between Olodumare and mankind. However, other legends tell a different story of an attentive deity who knows the affairs of man and the Orishas.

The Symbolic Meaning of Olodumare

The Yoruba people understand the god of the sky and the heavens, Olodumare, in many ways. He created the universe and all things in it and is the ultimate source of authority, law, and order. Therefore, he is considered the Supreme Being, who cannot be disobeyed. He is the fountain of wisdom, knowledge, and understanding. Through Olodumare, we learn and grow. He is the judge of all people, and he decides their fate after death. He is the one who gives out rewards and punishments and decides whether a person should be sent to heaven or hell after death.

How Did Olodumare Create the World?

African religions believe that creation occurred on different planets in various systems throughout the universe at different times. Several versions of this creation story depend on where a person lives. One of the most well-known is the spider and the palm tree story. In this story, Olodumare first created a spider. He told the spider to spin a web strong enough to hold up the world. The spider tried for a long time but could not do it. So, Olodumare killed him and used his remains to create a palm tree. Then, he told the palm tree to bend over and form the floor of the world. The tree bent down so far that it formed a bowl-like structure on the Earth's surface. Olodumare used water from the ocean to fill the bowl, forming the oceans and seas. He used a bit of soil to create dry land, which formed the continents. He used the palm tree's trunk to create the mountains and the tree's leaves to make the forests. Finally, he bent the tree's branches down to form the sky.

Another version of the creation story involves Obatala, the sky father. After the creation of the universe, there was only sky and water. Obatala wasn't satisfied with the creation of the universe and felt it was lacking. He went to Olodumare to ask permission to create dry land, and they obliged. With the help of other Orishas, Obatala obtained the necessary tools and descended to Earth to build hills, valleys, and mountains. He spent some time enjoying his new creation, but he became lonely and bored. He asked Olodumare's permission again to create mankind, and the deity agreed. After Obatala built humans, Olodunmare breathed life into them. Therefore, every living being possesses a part of the divine inside them.

Olodumare wasn't happy with the state of the world. He felt that something was missing. The world needed a positive force to bring joy and happiness, so he created Oshun, the Orisha of love.

The Orisa

The Yoruba believe Olodumare created spirits responsible for various aspects of life and the natural world. These spirits were called Orishas. These Orishas, like Oshu, Orunmila, and other gods, are intermediaries between mankind and Olodumare. They are responsible for maintaining harmony and order in the universe. The Orishas are also responsible for the well-being of the people of Earth and act as guardians, providing advice, healing, and other help to humans. What makes the Orishas particularly special is they were believed to have been human once. This is why they can understand human conditions and help humans when they are in need. Olodumare shares a special bond with the Orishas as he trusts them with the world's affairs. However, this trust was, at times, misplaced. The Orishas have plotted on more than one occasion to kill Olodumare.

What Religions Worship Olodumare

Many religions worship Olodumare. Some include the Yoruba religion, the Ifa religion, the Obeah religion, the African traditional religions, and the Caribbean religions. Also, many New Age religions worship Olodumare. For the Yoruba, Olodumare is the supreme deity. They believe he created the world and everything in it. He speaks to his followers through his priests and priestesses, known as Babalawos. They are trained in a divination system known as Ifa. The Ifa religion is a traditional religion that has been practiced in West Africa since ancient times. It is now primarily practiced in Nigeria, Ghana, Togo, and Benin. Ifa emphasizes the importance of nature and the environment and teaches that humans can live in harmony with the world by practicing a respectful way of life. The Obeah religion is an African traditional religion primarily practiced in Jamaica and other Caribbean islands. It combines the Yoruba religion and West African religious elements with Christianity and other influences. One of its central deities is Olodumare. The African traditional religions are related religions practiced in many African countries. Most worship Olodumare, but some also worship Orungan and Obatala.

How Do Followers Worship Olodumare?

Followers of Olodumare pray to him for guidance and to help them to live harmonious and compassionate lives. They often pray for healing and guidance in health-related issues. Although no specific shrines are dedicated to him (because he didn't come to earth, we don't know what he looks like), followers of Olodumare often create shrines dedicated to him and other Orishas. These shrines are usually found in people's houses who practice the Orisha religion. They will light candles, pour out libations, and pray to the Orishas. Often, they leave gifts, like sweets or flowers, as an offering to the Orishas. Some also offer animal sacrifices to their Orishas, but this is not a general practice.

How Do Followers Connect to Olodumare?

There are many ways to connect to Olodumare. One is to follow any of the religions that worship him. Another is to meditate on his name and ask to be guided by him. Other ways are praying to him or reading about his creation and deeds. You may feel disconnected from the divine if you feel something missing in your life, like not being fulfilled or happy. You don't have to go through life feeling like a part of you is missing. You can connect with the divine in many ways, but you should do whatever method works.

Bondye

In the beginning, there was darkness, chaos, and noise. We may not know how or when the world was created, but we do know that the Haitians had a lot to say about it. Since the Haitian religion is derived from a different culture and region, their supreme god's origin story differs from Olodumare. Bondye, also known as Gran Mèt or Grand Maître, is the supreme creator of all things. Our understanding of this Vodou deity is limited as most resources only give a general overview of his role in the Vodou ritual. However, with further research, you can understand why this complex belief system provides such rich symbolism for the followers.

Who Is Bondye?

The majority of Haitians practice Voodoo, a West African-based religion that combines elements of African spirituality and Catholicism. One of the most important figures in the Vodou pantheon is Bondye, a creator god who is often equated with God in Christianity or other religions. However, there is no devil equivalent. It is often depicted as an old man with a long beard and hair that extends to the ground. He is the source of all things and the benefactor of all humanity.

The Symbolic Meaning of Bondye

Bondye is often depicted with a conch shell symbolizing his voice, which he used to create the world. He has two other symbols; a jar of fire and a blue cross. Bondye's symbols represent his power to create life and light. His colors are black and white because darkness and light have opposite qualities representing the duality of all things.

Bondye's role is to create everything that exists in the world, including people, animals, and material things like plants and minerals. From his throne at the center of the world, he oversees all that happens on Earth, giving it shape and form by making it rain and giving life by giving the sunlight to shine upon it. When someone prays to him, they invoke his power so their wishes can come true.

Bondye is also considered a protector against evil forces like voodoo curses and an oracle who helps people communicate with spirits from beyond this world. In addition, he is a judge who decides who lives and dies on Earth for good or bad deeds done in life.

The name Bondye comes from the French words *bon* and *dye*, meaning "good god." Similar to Olodumare, Bondye isn't involved in the affairs of mankind, so he created the Lwas to assist and be an intermediary between him and humans. It could be that Bondye's lack of involvement is due to his disinterest. However, Bondye, like Olodumare, represents many complexities often associated with supreme deities. He is far too complicated for the human mind to interact with or grasp. He is beyond our understanding. So, he created the Lwas, who are simple yet divine entities. Lwas are imperfect beings with many flaws, just like humans. This begs the question, did Olodumare and Bondye create the Orishas and Lwas to be imperfect on purpose? The gods probably intended for the entities people interact with daily to be relatable.

How Did Bondye Create the World?

The first things Bondye created were spirits (Lwas). These were created to help guide people get through difficult times in life.

After creating spirits, Bondye created humans. When people were born, they came out from Bondye himself. People may have had different skin colors or facial features depending on which part of Bondye they came from.

Next, Bondye made Earth. He made plants grow from seeds and placed animals on the Earth. Then he created islands and mountains to protect his creations from demons and evil spirits. Finally, he turned himself into the night and spread darkness over everything to keep evil away.

When people worship Bondye, they believe they are taking part in a cosmic dance of creation. They are creating their own world with Bondye's help. Along with Bondye, the people who worship him are also participating in their world's creation. You are making your place to live where you can feel comfortable and safe.

Lwa

The spirits belonging to Bondye are different from the Orisha of Olodumare. For example, the Lwa are ancestors who were once human. The Orishas were gods and goddesses and separate beings from their followers.

This difference also includes creating Lwa or Loa, who embody Haitian values to share their wisdom with others. The Lwa are powerful healers and protectors. They help keep people safe and guide them on their path in life. For example, if someone is having a hard time at work or school, a spirit might come along with advice about how to deal with it or protect themselves from further harm. In addition, when someone is in danger, the spirit can help them find a way out of the situation or contact emergency services to help them escape as quickly as possible. Bondye spirits can also have different personalities. Some spirits have more power than others, but it all depends on your connection to that spirit and your willingness to work with and command it.

How Do Followers Worship Bondye?

Vodou ranges from simple activities like the performance of spirit possession to more complex rituals like the consecration of an altar or an offering for a specific Lwa (spirit). Followers worship Bondye through a series of rituals, often involving drumming, dancing, singing, and a trance-like state. During this ritual, followers can communicate with their ancestors' spirits and Bondye.

How Do Followers Connect to Bondye?

Haitian Vodou followers connect to their gods or ultimate power through various methods. In some cases, these methods reflect the religious beliefs of the follower, while in others, they may be more personal or idiosyncratic. Common methods include prayer and ritualized dancing, such as the sabbat. In addition, many Haitian Vodou practitioners use herbs and herbal remedies to connect with their gods. Depending on individual followers' needs, these methods can be used alone or combined with another. While no single method is inherently superior to another, each has advantages and disadvantages. Some are more effective for people at certain times, while others could have a more lasting impact on overall spiritual well-being.

Why Is Bondye Important?

The story behind Haitian Vodou's supreme creator, Bondye, is intriguing, complex, and of great importance to those following this religion. The creation story of Bondye and his two helpers is a beautiful example of how diverse cultures can blend together and produce something unique. Bondye is the supreme creator of all things, good and evil, to the Haitian Vodou followers. The story of his creation takes us back to a time when chaos reigned. It is a story of light emerging from darkness and order emerging from chaos.

Why Do These Religions Need a Supreme Creator?

African religions follow a supreme creator for several reasons, including that these religions were likely born out of a period of social disruption. In other words, they were created to preserve cultural identity. As people were moving around and changing their lifestyles, they had to devise new ways to explain who they were and where they came from. It's also possible that Africans were naturally more inclined to believe in a supreme Creator than their non-African counterparts. Even if this isn't true, it doesn't mean that belief in a supreme Creator doesn't make sense. African cultures have always been known for their strong spiritual beliefs and connection to the land. So, it makes sense for them to believe in something like a supreme Creator.

African religions follow a supreme god for several reasons:

- These religions emerged on the continent, and African people have an affinity for their ancestral gods
- Many African gods share similarities with other world religions, making them familiar and approachable
- These religions often have a large following across the continent, providing an anchor point for people to gather and organize

These are a few of the reasons African religions follow a supreme god. Others include space limitations, lack of familiarity with other deities, and cultural influences. All these factors significantly impacted African religious development.

The supreme creator god concept comes from African religions. Their beliefs center on a single god who created all things or a group of gods who are the highest and most powerful of their kind.

These supreme creator gods are much greater than humans and often have different names in different cultures. They're almost always separate from nature. They can continue to reside outside the natural world or simply be apart from it until they reclaim it again or send their followers back to it in the future.

Mankind owes everything to the supreme deities. They created the universe and breathed life into all living creatures. Although they exist far from the people, we can never accuse them of abandoning their creation. They left the world in the care of the Orishas and Lwas, who have never ceased to provide support and guidance. Whether the gods are involved or not, they exist in all their creations.

Chapter 4: The Lwa and the Orishas

As you learn more about African spiritual practices, the terms Lwa and Orishas will come up quite often. It's easy to confuse them since they share many similarities. However, there is one key difference separating the two. The Lwa are spirits in Voodoo and Haitian religions, while the Orishas are gods in the Yoruba religion. This chapter provides detailed information about the Lwa and the Orishas and their similarities and differences.

The Orishas are gods in the Yoruba religion.
Omoeko Media, CC BY-SA 4.0 <https://creativecommons.org/licenses/by-sa/4.0>, via Wikimedia Commons https://commons.wikimedia.org/wiki/File:Orishas_in_Oba%27s_palace,_Abeokuta.jpg

The Lwa

The word "Lwa" means spirits, but these entities are no ordinary spirits. They are divine beings who are significant in Voodoo and Haitian practices. However, unlike the Orishas, they aren't gods. The Lwas or Loas are intermediary spirits who travel between heaven and earth to deliver mankind's messages to Bondye, the creator god in Haitian and Voodoo religions. No one knows how many Loas exist. They could be infinite since there are ones we aren't aware of, but there are about a thousand Loas in Voodoo. They are divided into families, like the Guede, Petwo Lwa, and Rada Lwa. Each family differs in its music, rituals, offerings, and dances.

According to Haitian Voodoo beliefs, Loas are everywhere around us in the natural world. They exist in plants, mountains, rivers, trees, etc. Loas are helpful spirits associated with various aspects of nature, like wind and rain, and assist mankind in many daily activities like farming, fighting, and healing for the sick. However, they are more than just helpful spirits. They are powerful enough to change someone's destiny. They don't have a specific form since they are spirits. They usually appear to people by possessing a willing person during a ritual to interact with the attendees.

Some Loas were originally spirits of the dead, but many come from African gods and goddesses. They reside with the spirits of the dead in a place called the Vilokan. Legba, a prominent male Lwa, stands guard at the gates of the Vilokan. No one is allowed to communicate with a Lwa or any spirits in Vilokan without his permission. In Voodoo practices, practitioners call upon their Lwas to ask for help. They appease them by making various offerings like drinks or food.

During slavery and after the arrival of Christianity, enslaved people living in places like Louisiana and Haiti didn't abandon their pagan beliefs. They combined Lwas with some of the Catholic saints. Refusing to give up their religion was a form of rebellion against the oppression they faced. Holding on to their beliefs and history was their way of maintaining their identity.

Venerating Loas

Unlike Bondye, the Loas were more involved in people's daily lives. Although from the outside, the relationship between mankind and the Lwa seems demanding since humans serve them, it is still a very satisfying relationship. Loas significantly impact Voodoo practices, and serving them is one of the religion's main activities. Although the Loas are helpful and giving, they also have a dark side that can easily be avoided. Honoring the Loas and presenting them with offerings can protect you from their wrath and punishment. The relationship between Loas and humans is mutually beneficial. Humans present them with offerings and devotions, and the Loas provide humans with protection, favors, blessings, and healing.

Voodoo practitioners highly revere the Loas, which is clear from how they *call on them*. They give them the same respect given an elderly person by calling them "Manman," meaning mother, "Papa," meaning father, and "Metrès," meaning mistress. Practitioners hold specific ceremonies for Loas. These ceremonies have a religious nature and usually occur in a Voodoo temple led by a priest or a priestess.

The Loas ritual ceremonies usually involve drumming, dancing, songs, praying, and tracing the Veve. The Veves are specific rituals where the participants draw symbols called "Veve." There are as many Veves as there are Loas since each Loa has one symbol or more associated with it. The purpose of these ceremonies is to invite them to accept the offerings. When the Lwa arrives at the ceremony, it possesses the priest or the priestess leading the ritual. In some rare cases, it possesses one of the attendees. Possession allows the Loa to communicate with the worshipers. It is the perfect opportunity for them to ask their Loa questions or favors.

Possession isn't a negative experience or a forceful one like in the movies. The Loa don't mean any harm; it answers the people's calls and prayers and possesses a willing host. It provides guidance and healing. Since the word possession has a negative connotation, many people use the term "mount" instead.

The Pantheon of the Lwa

Loas are categorized into families with their characteristics and responsibilities. This part of the chapter focuses on the three most significant Loas families: Rada Lwa, Ghede Lwa, and Petro Lwa.

The Rada Lwa

The Rada Lwa originated in West Africa. It is a family of spirits or deities known for their creativity and calm and kind nature. Although the Rada Loas have a cool temper, some have similar aspects to the aggressive characteristics of the Petro Lwa. These Loas were highly revered among the enslaved people brought to America. Many Rada Loas were integrated into Christianity and associated with various saints.

One of the most significant figures in the Rada Lwa pantheon is Papa Legba. Although he is a very powerful spirit, he is known to be mischievous and a trickster that can even trick fate. People struggling with a difficult decision or requiring a change in their lives call upon Legba for guidance. All rituals should begin with invoking Legba since he is the gatekeeper of the supernatural world and the intermediary between mankind and the Loas. In some places in Africa, Legba is considered a fertility god. In others, he is the guardian of children. He is often associated with Saint Peter, the gatekeeper of Christianity's heaven.

Dambala is another prominent figure, and he is Legba's rival. According to African myth, Dambala was the first Lwa Bondye created, and he assisted Bondye with creating the universe. Hence, he is considered a father figure for mankind. His image is of a white serpent. Legends state that he shed his skin to create valleys and mountains. Dambala represents wisdom, healing magic, and knowledge. He lives between the sea and the earth and is also associated with Saint Patrick.

Erzulie is a female Lwa associated with the colors pink and blue. She is the goddess of love and beauty and symbolizes sensuality and femininity. She is invoked by women struggling with issues related to feminine sexuality or motherhood. Erzulie is associated with the Christianity theme Lady of Sorrows because she is constantly grieving for what she can't have and often weeps at the end of rituals.

Loco, the patron of healers, and his wife Ayizan, the ruler of commerce, are considered prominent Loas in the Rada Loa pantheon. They are the parents of the spiritual priesthood since they were the first priest and priestesses.

Ghede Lwa

The Ghede Lwa pantheon is associated with sexual desire and death. They are responsible for delivering the spirits of the dead to the underworld. These Loas are known for their obscene behavior, like making inappropriate jokes or provocative dance moves. Although they are associated with death, they are known for enjoying and celebrating life.

Baron Samedi is the superior Lwa of the Ghede Lwa pantheon. He is the Lwa of death and is extremely powerful. He greets the spirits of the dead and guides them on their journey to the other world. Baron Samedi is depicted as a corpse covered in black cloth, which is the traditional Haitian burial custom. He is the protector of cemeteries and is highly revered yet feared among Voodoo followers. Similar to his family, Baron Samedi enjoys swearing, making crude jokes, drinking, and smoking. He is known for his multiple affairs with mortal women, even though he is married to the female Lwa Manman Brigitte. He doesn't only help the dead but the living, too. He can lift curses, heal the sick, and resurrect the dead. People invoke him to help the sick and dying.

Petro Lwa

Petro or Petwo Lwa isn't as old as the other families since they originated from Haiti. They are the hot-tempered and aggressive Loas, unlike the Rada and Gehde. For this reason, they can be invoked for dark practices and magic. Categorizing Petro Lwa as evil may be naive since many of its Loas are invoked in rituals to provide assistance rather than harm.

The Orishas

The Orishas or Orisas are minor deities or spirits from the Yoruba religion. Similar to the Loas, they act as mediators between the Yoruba supreme god Olodumare and mankind. Like in Voodoo, the supreme deity isn't directly involved with people and their affairs. It is the Orishas who assist them in their daily activities. The simple human mind will never comprehend the complexity of Olodumare, so he created the Orishas as different aspects of himself. There aren't as many Orishas as there are Loas since there are only 401 Orishas. When enslaved people of Yoruba reached America and were introduced to Christianity, they combined the Orishas with Catholic

Christian saints, like the Loas.

For this reason, countries like Brazil and Cuba refer to Orishas as Saints or Santos. Another similarity with the Loas is that many Orishas were once the spirits of the dead. However, these were the spirits of wise and intellectual individuals.

Practitioners invoke the Orishas to seek guidance, assistance, and enlightenment. Many people worldwide, like Wiccans, Neo-Pagans, and Santeria followers, worship the Orishas and incorporate them into their rituals. Orishas are depicted in human forms and can appear to people through possessions like the Loas.

The main purpose of Orishas is to assist mankind without selfish gain. However, Orishas have a personality and characteristics with strengths and weaknesses, which make them closer to humans than gods. As a result, they defy their purpose, and instead of assisting, they focus on their own personal gains. Neither mankind nor the Orishas are perfect, and they can succumb to their dark side and become arrogant, envious, or proud. In one legend, the Orishas rebelled against Olodumare by refusing to follow his orders because they believed they should rule the universe since they were more involved in mankind's affairs. When Olodumare found out, he stopped the rain, causing drought and death to the lands and crops. This was a tough lesson for the Orishas, who repented and begged Olodumare for forgiveness. Although their human-like qualities got them into trouble with Olodumare, these qualities made them relatable among practitioners. They aren't perfect beings detached from humanity. They are flawed, making it easy for people to identify and sympathize with them.

Similar to Loas, the Orishas exist in nature and accept offerings of food and drinks. Each Orisha is associated with a color and number and has favorite offerings. By understanding the Orishas and their personalities, you can tailor the right offering to each so they can recognize it. Orishas rule over nature, and you can learn about their personalities and temperament by watching the force of nature they represent.

Venerating the Orishas

Rituals that involve dancing and drumming help practitioners communicate with Orishas. Similar to Lwa, an Orisha will mount the priest leading the ritual, referred to as trance possession. Trance possession is largely significant in venerating the Orishas in the Santeria religion. A ceremony is held for the Orishas, called a bembé (drumming party). The purpose of these ceremonies is the same as the Loas' - to invite an Orisha to mount any attending priests.

Specific songs and dances are performed during these ceremonies to entice the Orisha to join. Whoever the Orisha chooses to mount is considered a great honor and a blessing for this person. Like Loas, Orishas only mount priests or priestesses. However, if they mount (possess) one of the attendees, it strongly signifies that this person should become a priest or priestess. During trance possession, attendees can communicate with the Orisha. Mounting is a joyful experience that leaves the person wiser and in awe of being the host to such a powerful being.

You can revere Orishas and Loas together or only the Orishas since they can replace the Loas in many rituals.

The Pantheon of the Orishas

Unlike the Loas, the pantheon of the Orishas looks different since they aren't categorized into families. This part of the chapter focuses on the most significant Orishas in Yoruba and Sanitaria.

Eshu

Eshu or Elegba, similar to Papa Legba, is the god of trickery and mischief. He has the same powers as the Norse god Loki, but Eshu isn't as evil as his counterpart and doesn't harm mankind or other gods. He acts as a messenger between mankind and the spirit world. Eshu is favored by Olodumare since he helped him during the Orisha rebellion. Eshu was the one who told Olodumare the Orishas weren't following his orders. In another story, Olodumare is terrified of mice, so the Orishas decide to take advantage of this weakness and scare him to death so they could rule in his place. Their plan almost worked, but Eshu interfered and rescued Olodumare, who punished the Orishas involved and rewarded Eshu. Eshu's reward was to do whatever he wanted with no consequences to his actions, allowing him the freedom to perform many tricks and pranks.

Shango

Like the Norse god Thor, Shango or Chango in Santeria is the god of Thunder. He controls lightning and thunder and is associated with magic, masculinity, and sexuality. He is married to three Orishas; Oba, Oya, and Oshun. Practitioners call upon him to lift hexes and curses. He is associated with Saint Barbra in Christianity.

Oya

Oya is the protector of the dead and is associated with cemeteries, ancestors, and the weather. She rules over all the dead, including animals and plants. Oya is the goddess of change and, like the weather, is constantly changing and never remains in the same state for long. Oya is also a fierce warrior, often fighting by her husband's side in battle. She is tied with Saint Teresa in Christianity.

Oshun

Oshun is the Orisha of the rivers, fertility, love, and marriage. She governs all relationships and is associated with genitals and feminine beauty. Oshun's role was crucial in the legend when Olodumare caused drought in response to the Orishas' rebellion. The Orishas repented for their actions and wept to beg Olodumare to bring back the rain. However, their voices never reached him. Oshun decided to deliver the Orishas' repentance message to Olodumare and beg him to forgive them. She transformed into a peacock and took a long journey to Olodumare. However, she flew too close to the sun and burned her wings. She succeeded in delivering the message even though she lost her wings and fell sick. Olodumare was impressed by her courage and persistence, healed her, and replaced her burned peacock wings with the wings of a vulture. He bestowed an honor upon her by making her the only Orisha to deliver him messages. Oshun corresponds with Our Lady of Charity, an aspect of the Virgin Mary.

Orunmila

Ornumilla or Ornula is the Orisha of wisdom, knowledge, and divination. He is the only Orisha who doesn't interact with mankind through Terrance's possession or mounting. Practitioners communicate with him through divination. Ornumilla is one of the oldest Orishas and has been around since the beginning of time and witnessed the creation of mankind. Therefore, he knows the fate of mankind and each soul's past, present, and future. Practitioners invoke Ornumilla to gain insight into what the future holds and to learn if their actions will help them to achieve their destiny. He is associated with St. Joseph, St. Philip, and St. Francis of Assisi in

Christianity.

Yemaya

Yemaya is the protector of women and the Orisha of seas, mystery, and lakes. She is regarded as a mother figure since she is associated with motherhood. She is the mother of the Orishas, so she is one of the most revered Orishas in the pantheon. She resembles Our Lady of Regala from Catholic Christianity.

Osain

Osain is the god of nature. He governs the forests and has powers over herbs giving him the power to heal. He is the protector of homes and is associated with hunting. Osain used to look like a regular man, but after he lost an eye, ear, leg, and arm, he looked like a cyclops with his other eye in the center of his forehead. He also uses a tree branch to help him walk. He is associated with several Christian saints like St. Joseph, St. John, St. Benito, and St. Ambrose.

Obaluaye

Obaluaye is the god of miracles and healing. Although he is a healer, Obaluaye also has the power to curse people. Hence, people are terrified and respect him. Practitioners invoke him to heal the sick, especially those gravely ill.

Oba

Oba is the Orisha of rivers, and she symbolizes water. She represents energy, flexibility, manifestation, restoration, movement, and protection. She is Yemaya's daughter and one of Shango's three wives. Oba is responsible for the flow of time, which is why people turn to her when they feel stagnant and unable to achieve their goals. Oba and her sisters Oya and Oshun provide safe waters to the people they need to survive. In some places in Africa, she is the protector of prostitutes, and in Brazil, she is the Orisha of love.

The Loas and Orishas are more alike than they are different. They have human qualities and aren't regarded as perfect beings who can do no wrong. Both entities are relatable because they are guided by their emotions and have weaknesses that can get them into trouble. People feel close to them because, like us, they also suffer, struggle, fall, and get up again.

Both entities were created to help and serve humans, so they deserve to be highly revered. They must always be acknowledged for their existence and show gratitude to ensure their blessings' continuation. The Orishas and Loas need humans just as humans need them. People need assistance from the Lwa and Orishas daily; these entities depend on human acknowledgment and offerings to survive.

Chapter 5: Santeria and the Saints

Due to the similarities between the Orisha's worship and the representation of its saints, Santeria is often compared to its parent religion, Yoruba. However, unlike the Yoruba traditions regarding deities, Santeria's religious syncretism means that spirits are represented by Catholic saints. After colonization, enslaved people brought to the New World were forced to convert to Christianity. However, because there were many similarities between the deities of African religions and Christian saints, the enslaved people could maintain their beliefs by merely renaming their gods. They could continue worshiping them and also created another religion called Santeria. This chapter is dedicated to Santeria, its saints, and how they are celebrated through their different correspondences.

Santeria worship can be done through an altar or symbolization with a statue or doll.
Ji-Elle, CC BY-SA 4.0 <https://creativecommons.org/licenses/by-sa/4.0>, via Wikimedia Commons https://commons.wikimedia.org/wiki/File:Trinidad-Santer%C3%ADa_(1).jpg

What Is Santeria?

Santeria is a religion born out of a combination of an African religion called "Regla Ocha de Los Yorubas" and Catholicism. Due to this, it accepts and mixes rigorous Christian traditions and free-flowing pagan Yoruba practices. Santeria means "The way of the saints" or the "the way of worshiping the saints." The saints in question are also identified as Orishas or Lwas in different African religions. However, the Orishas and the spirits (Lwas and the Santeria saints) are viewed differently, which is notable in how they are worshiped. Where Orishas are depicted as deities who only answer to the Supreme Being, the spirits have no divine qualities.

Santeria encompasses two main concepts, Ache (the divine power) and ebbo (sacrifice). By connecting with Ache, practitioners can achieve any spiritual goals. Most Santeria rituals help obtain Ache, which, in turn, helps find answers to questions, guidance, or whatever you need. On the other hand, ebbo is a sacrifice made to the Orishas (saints) when asking them for a specific favor. These favors are usually related to witchcraft and ailments. The offerings include flowers, candles, fruit, and other food and drink.

Santeria is a unique system, as it represents a decentralized religion, meaning practitioners have no specific places for worship. There are no predetermined ways to honor the deities, doctrines to follow, or rules to conduct rituals. When a practitioner has a need, they call on a saint (Orisha) and ask for guidance, assistance, or whatever they require. They also offer gratitude or make sacrifices and offerings before and after receiving the blessings. How this is done can differ from one practitioner to another, indicating that it's a highly intuitive practice.

Apart from worshiping the saints, followers of Santeria also practice ancestral veneration and believe there is a possibility to communicate with ancestral spirits and the different forces of nature. Whether you want to evoke a saint, ancestral, or other spirits, the best way is through an altar dressed for the occasion. A symbol of the saint is needed when calling on them. It can be a picture or a statute. The altar is covered with a cloth in the color associated with the saint. The other elements (candles, elements of nature, offerings symbols) are linked to the Orisha. If you're addressing another spirit, like the ancestors, the altar is dressed in their favorite colors, offerings, and symbols.

The Saints of Santeria

While the number of saints (deities) you can work with in Santeria practices is vast, a few can be particularly helpful for beginners. Below, you'll find a few you can connect with. You must approach them respectfully and follow through by thanking them when receiving their help. If you aren't sure which saint you should contact, meditate with their symbols to see which resonates with you. Reading about their powers can help determine who can assist you with your needs or requests. Once you've found the entity whose power you need to connect with, prepare to approach them. Working with Santeria saints requires practice. You need to get close to them to understand them. Understanding them will help you prepare adequate offerings, please them, and harness their power to uncover higher wisdom.

Mary - Yemaya

Known as Yemalla and the Star of the Sea, Yemaya represents the Santerian aspect of the divine trinity. She is the goddess of salty waters, where life comes from, so she is considered the mother of the world. Yemaya also rules over the moon and guides the sailors and fishermen traveling through the seas and oceans. The goddess is associated with witchcraft, fertility, children, and women. She represents the Virgin Mary and is often called Our Lady of Rule in prayers.

Besides prayers, Mary can be invoked through meditation, visualization, and several other techniques when you need help with fertility issues, pregnancy, and children's illnesses. She can accompany you on a journey across the sea or ocean and grant you safe travel. Invoke Yemaya on the Saturday before your trip to ensure the best results. Her colors are white and blue, so use these to decorate your altar and wear them on your travels. Using white and blue crystal beads, you can make a charm that harnesses Yemaya's protective powers.

You can perform several rituals to call on Yemaya - use them for meditation, affirmation, or when asking for help, guidance, or healing. Here is a simple one:

- Make an offering of fruit - bananas, pineapples, and other tropical fruit work best, but you can also use whatever is in season

- Place the offering in a bowl (or large seashell if you can find one) on your altar

- Put a bowl of salty water next to the offering

- Place seven coins around the bowls in a circle. These represent how many days are between the moon's two phases

- Look at the water, and say the following:

   "Mary, you are grace,

   You're enlightenment,

   You are blessed among women,

   And so is the fruit of your womb.

   Bless me, mother of all

   Help me now throughout this journey."

- Practitioners often combine a similar version of the prayer to Mary (Hail Mary) with a rosary. If you feel comfortable, you can repeat this prayer several times using rosary beads.

- When you have finished with this prayer, in your words, tell the goddess what help you need

- End with an expression of gratitude for granting her power

Las Mercedes - Obatala

As the second aspect of the divine trinity, Obatala represents the male counterpart of Mary. Known as Our Lady of Mercy, Obatala was the one who brought life to earth. He was the first saint (deity) ever created by Olodumare, implying that he is the wisest of all. He can chase away negative energies and protect the fathers, just as Yemaya protects mothers and their children.

Obatala's color is white, meaning any offerings and representations would be presented in this color. Traditional offerings to this deity include rice, milk, coconut, yams, cascarilla, white hens and doves, and cotton. Offerings made and prayers requesting assistance should be recited on Sunday.

Calling on Obatala is helpful when you need to communicate your negative feelings toward others or eliminate negativity from your life. Using a white, seven-day candle will ensure you acquire purity in mind and body and obtain your goals.

You need the following:

- Yams
- Rice
- Milk
- Coconut shavings
- Cascarilla - fresh or dry
- A piece of white cotton yarn
- A white, seven-day candle
- A representation of the saint

Instructions:

1. Organize your altar or sacred space by clearing away anything not required for this ritual.
2. Place the white candle and a symbol representing Obatala onto your altar.
3. Prepare the rice, milk, coconut, and yams in separate bowls and place them on the altar.
4. If using fresh or whole dried cascarilla, tie the plant into a bunch with white cotton yarn.
5. If using chopped dry leaves, spread them around the candle and tie the yarn around the bottom of the candle.
6. When ready, light the candle, close your eyes, and prepare to call on Our Lady of Mercy.

   Then, recite the following spell:

   "Oh great Lady of Mercy, please lend me your power,

   Send me patience and knowledge.

   May I be strong and wise,

   So I can pursue my passions.

   Help me stay fair and caring,

   To treat others with great integrity."

7. The candle should burn for seven days. The best practice is to leave it burning only during the time you can supervise it and focus on gathering the saint's energy.

8. Snuff the candle out when you have finished your prayer and go about your day. Relight it when you can supervise it until it burns out.

Saint Barbara - Chango

Representing the third aspect of the divine trinity is Chango, the patron of transformation, fire, and merriment. He rules over thunder and lighting, through which he provides immense power. Saint Barbara was an innocent young woman who became the protector of souls who suffered wrongful deaths after being killed by her father when she converted to Christianity. Chango is a spirit who empowers people seeking revenge or wanting to take back something stolen from them. According to the lore, her father was struck by lightning when Saint Barbara died. Hence the connection between this seemingly unlikely pairing.

Chango's colors are white and red. Friday is the best day to pray to her or ask for her assistance. On this day, you can reclaim your power using Chango's power. Here is a practice to help you with this endeavor.

You'll need the following:

- Red and white prayer beads (98 in total)
- Paper and pen
- Red candle

Instructions:

1. Make a ring of the beads, starting with a white stone. Then add six red ones, followed by six white ones, and finish the sequence with a red one.

2. Repeat the pattern six times.

3. Write affirmations for each bead on the ring. Ensure they are positive statements and write them in the present tense as if you already had whatever you wished for.

4. Adorn your altar using white and red decorations, Saint Barbara symbols, swords, lightning bolts, a cup, and a red candle.

5. On a Friday night, light the candle and say as many affirmations as you can while remaining focused and counting down the beads.

6. Repeat the steps for 24 consecutive Fridays leaving offerings of apples, bananas, anise, red okra, and red wine to Chango.

Saint Anthony - Eleggua

Whereas Eleggua is the messenger of the deities in the Yoruba pantheon, Saint Anthony reconciles people who have lost touch or had a disagreement with each other. Eleggua can open the door to divine wisdom and make people hear what they would otherwise miss. Before invoking another saint, you must first call on Saint Anthony (Eleggua) to ensure your message will be sent. For example, you can say:

> *"Eleggua, I ask you to open the doors for me,*
>
> *To remove the barrier between this world and the spiritual realm*
>
> *So I can pass my message through."*

Since Eleggua is also linked to protection, you can harness his power to ward off negative energies. His colors are red and black, so use beads, flowers, or decorations in this color to make a charm or talisman. Place this on your front door to protect your home, or take it with you to safeguard your person.

You can also offer rum, cigars, coconut, smoked fish, other red and white food and drink, candy, and toys on Mondays to evoke Eleggua. It will come in handy if you need a specific favor.

You need the following:

- A brown candle
- A representation of the saint or deity
- An assortment of canned food

Instructions:

1. Start by lighting the candle and saying the following:

> *"Saint Anthony, you who are always ready to help those in trouble,*
>
> *I ask you to empower me with what I need to do.*
>
> *My request may be grand, but I have faith in you.*

Please grant me this favor, and I will be eternally grateful."

2. Visualize your message being carried upward through the candle smoke and traveling toward the spiritual realm.

3. Let the candle burn out, take the canned food and offer it to someone in need, whether a food bank or a specific person.

Saint Joseph - Osain

The husband of Mary, Saint Joseph, has a clear connection to Osain, the nature god of the Yoruba. Despite often depicted as a frail person relying on a crutch, Saint Joseph can be a powerful ally. He answers all the prayers dedicated to him, especially if coming from the heart. He is the patron of homes, carpenters, other hand laborers, fathers, those who die happy, and parents who take in children needing a loving home.

Osain is associated with nature and the forest and empowers healing herbs. According to Santeria, if you pray to him while foraging, he will help you find the plants to ward off evil spirits and their effects. However, Saint Joseph oversees everything vulnerable, so you must ask his permission before removing any plant or herb from its natural habitat.

A ritual performed in the name of Saint Joseph can help grant his ashe to assist you in protection or healing. He favors the color yellow, and offering food and other items in this color on a Thursday makes the ritual even more powerful.

For this ritual, you need the following:

- A yellow candle
- Pine incense (to represent nature)
- A symbol (picture or statute) of Saint Joseph
- Plant parts you find in a forest, like pine cones, cedar needles, blackberry thorns, etc.
- A small bag

Instructions:

1. Place the candle and the incense on your altar in front of the symbol and light them.

2. Take the symbol into your hands, and move it over the incense smoke while saying:

"By the power of this candle's fire and the smoke of pine

May my home be protected from evil spirits.

Saint Joseph, please heed my prayer.

As all green things grow

And heal with your help,

May I be guarded by your ashe

Please protect my home and those who are inside."

3. Place the plant parts into the bag, and finish the ritual with this prayer:

"Our protector, Saint Joseph,

Grant me relief from spiritual harm

I implore you to protect this home from evil."

4. Place the bag with the plant parts in front of your home by hanging it up or burning it partially in the ground to secure it in place.

Our Lady of Charity - Oshun

Also known as the Our Lady of Caridad del Cobre, Oshun is one of the most influential saints and deities. She is the goddess of love, fertility, rebirth, renewal, pleasure, marriage, sexuality, art, and finances. Oshun can grant you fertility in all areas of life and is known to be very charitable, which explains why she is linked to Our Lady of Charity.

Oshun is often evoked on Fridays. However, she is the most powerful on September 8 and celebrated with an enormous feast on this day. Despite being compassionate, she can be easily angered. To avoid making her lose her temper, she must be appeased regularly. She loves gold and lavish decorations, so if you want to address her, this is how you should adorn your altar. Gold-colored jewelry, gold, yellow or white candles, honey, white wine, rum cakes, pumpkins, and other yellow and white fruit and vegetables are her favorites.

Perform this ritual for Our Lady of Charity to attract love and prosperity.

You need the following:

- A piece of jewelry
- A nice metal dish

- A yellow or gold candle
- Honey
- A representation of the saint
- A piece of yellow cloth
- Paper and pen

Instructions:

1. Arrange the jewelry in the dish on your altar in front of the saint's representation.
2. Pour the honey over the jewelry and light the candle.
3. Focus on your intention and meditate on it. Think about why you want to attract that specific thing.
4. Extinguish the candle and go to sleep.
5. When you wake up the following morning, wrap the jewelry in a yellow cloth and pray to Oshun.
6. Next, write five lines reaffirming your intention (the reasons you decided on the previous night).
7. Fold the paper five times and place it beneath the candle used the previous night.
8. Light the candle again and offer another prayer to Oshun.
9. When you've finished, extinguish the candle.
10. Repeat the last step for five days, burn the paper, and bury its ashes in your garden or in a pot.
11. Be sure to thank the saint when your wishes have been granted.

Saint Peter - Oggun

Like Saint Peter is asked for help when a person needs work or wants to be successful in their workplace, Oggun provides the ashe for hard-working people. If you're willing to put in the effort, he will help you reach your professional goals. He is associated with the colors green and black. If you want to realize a new business venture or manifest a better job, adorn your altar with these colors. The best day to pray to Saint Peter is Tuesday. The best offerings for him are green food, rum, cigars, green leaves, and "hard-working" animals like a rooster that gets up early in the morning. Oggun is connected to the earth element, so you can use soil in your rituals.

For a simple ritual invoking Saint Peter, you need the following:

- A symbol of Saint Peter
- An iron cauldron or bowl
- Two keys (symbolizes the saint and the deity)
- Seven other pieces of iron (nails, small tools, etc.)
- Black and green cloth for the altar
- Black and green beads
- String
- Offerings of your choice
- Paper and pen

Instructions:

1. Make a circlet of the string and beads, starting with a black stone. Follow up with seven green beads, add seven black ones, and finish the sequence with a green one.
2. Repeat six times to have 112 beads on the circlet.
3. Write your intention on the paper, and tuck the paper under the green candle you placed on your altar.
4. Light the candle, and pray to Saint Joseph while visualizing your goal and going through the beads.
5. When you've finished, snuff out the candle and bury the paper in the soil.

The Santeria religion includes many saints represented by Catholic saints. These saints are of the highest order and demand due respect. So, whenever you invoke them for favors or questions, you must do so with the utmost respect and gratitude.

Chapter 6: Honor Thy Ancestors

Ancestral veneration is a practice shared by various cultures. People who honor their ancestors through spiritual practices believe their loved ones exist in another realm. Most humans are only capable of seeing what is in the physical realm, and not everyone can witness spirits who have crossed the physical realm.

Honoring the ancestors is an integral part of African spirituality.
https://unsplash.com/photos/n_GkKJCGgBI

Therefore, people communicate with their ancestors through spiritual means. Of course, there are other reasons why honoring ancestors is a vital practice. This chapter thoroughly explains the nature of ancestral worship, how different spiritual practices view the ancestors, and how and why they honor them.

Ancestors: Who Are They? Why Should We Honor Them?

Defining the word "ancestors" may seem a bit absurd, but it is crucial to understand ancestral veneration truly.

When the word "ancestors" is mentioned, most people think of the family members who came before them; grandparents, great-grandparents, etc. In a strictly biological sense, to an extent, this is true. Your ancestors are the people who came before you and with whom you share a connection by blood.

However, the definition of ancestors becomes less about blood and more about connection with spiritual practices. It includes all connections made throughout a person's life, spiritual connections, connections made with guides or mentors, connections with loved ones, friends, and blood relatives.

Of course, some practitioners firmly believe that only blood relatives count as ancestors. There are no rigid rules in spirituality. Ultimately, it's about what aligns best with the practitioner.

According to African Theology, man is not just flesh. Humans have three layers, Ma, Ka, and Ba. Ma is the body, Ka is the energy force that moves the body, and Ba is the soul. However, when the body completes its earthly cycle, the soul is separated from it and returns to its divine realm. The soul of the physically dead person is still around, and you can communicate with it.

Honoring the dead is part of African culture. It is deeply ingrained. It is reflected in their spiritual practices regardless of how they vary. Dedicating specific days or hours to the ancestors is a celebration of their lives. It is how we pay respect to and honor them.

Ancestors are seen as protectors and wisdom givers. Many believe ancestors can help from the beyond. Their help can be whatever you need it to be. Are you looking to answer questions you do not have answers for? Ask your ancestors. Do you need guidance with a certain situation? Pray for your ancestors to guide you. Are you having trouble with your life lately? Ask your ancestors to help you through this difficult time.

The ancestors are perceived as divine and loving figures. They love you, and they watch over you from another realm. Trust that they have your best interest at heart. They will offer you wisdom and guidance whenever you need it.

So, it is important to keep up communication with your ancestors. Celebrating them on certain days shows you honor and respect them. It shows you appreciate what they do for you and that you are grateful. Honoring the ancestors on specific days or frequently communicating with them builds a strong relationship with them. The more you communicate or pray to your ancestors, the stronger you feel them around you. You'll feel their presence around you and feel their protection and warm embrace around you.

It is important to clarify that every African culture has its own way of honoring spirits from beyond. African spirituality is mostly viewed as a closed practice, meaning only people with African roots can engage in these practices. This also applies to practices within the culture. If you practice Haitian Voodoo, it may be best to honor your ancestors according to your beliefs.

However, some practices like Hoodoo and Haitian Voodoo allow outsiders to practice their beliefs and rituals. This only happens through a process of initiation conducted by certain priests. If you are not a member of either practice but feel connected to their teachings and rituals, it is best to research and consult the priests before joining. It is also vital to remain polite and respectful when addressing the priests. After all, these faiths are highly regarded and valued, so always be respectful.

Yoruba

Individuals who live according to the Yoruba religion, called Isese, have shrines for their ancestors. The ancestors can be related to you through blood, land, or history. Building a shrine or an altar is essential to connect with your ancestors. You'll go to the shrine whenever you need to pray for advice or guidance, as this is the designated meeting place you built for your spirit guides.

To build a shrine, you must first choose a surface. You can use a clean table or anything that can be used as a table top. It is preferable to place this table somewhere private in your apartment or home. You do not want interruptions when you are engaging with the energies.

You can place anything on it which is related to your ancestors when they were alive. It could be a piece of clothing, their favorite flower, leaves, pictures, etc. Place a clay plate or a seashell containing leaves or herbs.

Cleansing the altar physically and spiritually is vital. The place must be free of dust or clutter. It is considered disrespectful when the altar is placed in a dirty area. Spiritually cleansing the altar requires sage smoke or rosemary smoke. Set your heart and intentions in the right place as you energetically cleanse the altar. You must believe the smoke is getting rid of any wanted energies and is welcoming the spirits into a purified space. The spiritual cleansing must occur before and after your prayers.

It is also vital that you give offerings to the ancestors. The offerings could be as simple as a bowl of fruits, a white, lit candle, a cup of water, oils, etc. When you make offerings, you show appreciation and gratitude to the spirits. The offerings must proceed with a prayer. The prayer invites the spirits and lets them know these offerings are for them.

> *"E nle oo rami o. I am greeting you, my friends.*
>
> *Be ekolo ba juba ile a lanu. If the earthworm pays homage to the earth, the earth always gives it access.*
>
> *Omode ki ijuba ki iba pa a. A child who pays homage never suffers the consequences.*
>
> *Egun mo ki e o. Ancestors, I greet you.*
>
> *Egun mo ki e o ike eye. Ancestors, I greet you with respect.*
>
> *Ohun ti wu ba njhe lajule Orun. Whatever good things are being eaten in the realm of the ancestors.*
>
> *No mo ba won je. Eat my offering with them.*
>
> *J'epo a t'ayie sola n'igbale. Eat richly from the earth.*
>
> *Omo a t'ayie sola n-igbale. The children of the earth are grateful for your blessing.*
>
> *Ori Egun, mo dupe. I thank the wisdom of the ancestors.*
>
> *Ase. May it be so."*

When you need guidance from the spirits, you must pray to them first. The prayer is done over the shrine and is part of the cleansing ritual. The prayer is said over the leaves to bless them.

"Iba se Egun. I pay homage to the Spirit of the Ancestors

Emi (your name) Omo (list your lineage starting with your parents and working backward). I am (your name), child of (lineage)

Iba se Ori Ewe. I pay homage to the Spirit of the Leaves

Ko si 'ku. Send away the Spirit of Death

Ko si arun. Send away illness

Ko si wahala. Send away all gossip

Ase. May it be so."

Burn the leaves over the shrine. The smoke can also be used to cleanse yourself. Guide the smoke to move from your feet to your head. When you feel the smoke has cleansed the shrine, say, "toe," which means enough.

Yoruba priests advise the people only to invite specific spirits to the shrine. They typically avoid inviting ancestors who struggled with or exhibited addictive behavior. The same goes for ancestors who engaged in any form of abuse. Yoruba priests say their energies could cause unwanted problems for the person who prays to them.

Finally, you must seal the shrine with a fragrance you often wear mixed with your saliva or bodily fluid belonging to you. This lets the spirits know you are at the shrine they are being invited to. When done, ask the spirits for guidance or do readings to receive answers from them.

Santeria

Santeria is similar to the Yoruba religion. People who practice Santeria also build a shrine to their ancestors. The components may be different, but the rituals are similar. Like Isese, Santeria originated in Nigeria, but it is practiced more in Cuba and the United States.

The word 'Santeria' is translated as *"the way of the saints."* The saints refer to the Orishas, known as African spirits or deities. Santeria revolves around praying to the saints and constantly honoring them. So, building a shrine to honor them is a vital step.

In Santeria, ancestors are referred to as Egun. An Egun can be related to people by blood or religion, meaning you do not have to limit your prayers to your family ancestors. You can pray to any ancestor who practiced Santeria. The shrine should include two main ingredients, sticks and offerings.

The sticks you place on your shrine come from a specific tree the priests have blessed. Ask your priest and receive nine sticks from them. Tie the nine sticks with a red cloth and place them on the altar.

Next, place the offering. The offering can be an animal sacrifice, food, or drink. All offerings must be placed around the sticks. If you are invoking a spirit, you must use an Opa egun – a straight, tall stick taken from a tree. If you are to summon a spirit, you must be male and slowly tap the floor with the stick to catch the ancestor's attention, and they can hear your prayers.

Eating after you have made your offerings is important when offering food and drink to the spirit. Otherwise, it is considered disrespectful. The offerings should always contain food and drink. The drink could be water or any alcohol or liquor. It is also tradition to sprinkle water or liquor on the shrine through the lips or fingertips.

Certain ceremonies must be conducted to honor the ancestors in Santeria. The ceremony takes a few days to complete. On the first day, people offer large quantities of cooked meals, animal offerings, and drinks. People also sing and dance to their ancestors. People sing, dance, and play drums on the second day to honor the spirits. Food is also served on that day.

During the ceremonies, the following prayer is said if a member wants to connect to their ancestor. The spirit of the ancestors mounts (or possesses) the mediums gently while a vulture flies over the ceremony like a snake. The ancestors possess power beyond the realms of death. We must sweep and clean the ground before greeting our ancestors upon their arrival.

> *"The spirit of death directs our Ori toward the ancestors who have obtained the secret of life beyond death. Today, I show the marks of my body as a hymn to the sacred oath. I offer my devotion to the ancestors through the oath. And I am blessed by your energy and your wisdom. Ashe."*

Fét Gede in Haitian Voodoo

Fét Gede, or Festival day of the dead, is an important celebration dedicated to honoring the ancestors. Haitian Voodoo believes the spirits are not seen on any other day and only appear during their ceremony.

The Gede or ancestor can be a close friend or a family member. During a ceremony, the Voodooist or Voodoo practitioner invokes their spirit and turns them into a Gede.

This festival happens every November first and second. It is usually conducted in the cemetery, and, like Santeria, it involves a lot of singing and dancing. The Gede may possess individuals during the festival.

If an individual is possessed, they will immediately be recognized because of their physical appearance. They usually dress their faces with white powder and may wear black sunglasses, and have a walking staff. They also wear purple, black, and white clothing. They drink alcoholic beverages infused with hot peppers since the Gede love spicy peppers. Many will eat or apply hot peppers to their skin during the festival.

The possessions are another way to honor the dead. It is one way, Voodooists show the spirits they are welcomed into their world, space, and bodies. Ideally, Gedes do not have bad intentions toward their person, so usually, no harm is done during the possession.

The possession also shows the strong bond between the person and Gede. Of course, not everyone is comfortable with possessions, but they are practiced, nonetheless. If you are interested in having this bond with your Gede, ask your priest to learn more.

Like Santeria and Isese, Haitian Voodooists offer food and drinks to their ancestors. The offerings must be placed on a table in the cemetery to honor and respect those who have passed to the spiritual realm.

The Haitian Voodoo celebration of the dead is similar to Santeria since they dance, sing, and drum to the dead. The priests also pay respects and eat the food offered to the dead. Unlike Santeria and Isese, possessions occur on the day of the festival.

The ceremony cannot be conducted unless permission is granted from Papa Gede, the first man ever to die. Once priests have permission to conduct the ceremony, the celebrations begin.

Hoodoo

Hoodoo is similar to Isese and honors the ancestors. A clean shrine must be established in a neat environment. It must be cleansed with salt water or sage smoke. The altar must have pictures of the ancestors or any item connected to them. Hoodoos communicate with their ancestors frequently.

Their communications can be through prayers or normal conversations. Of course, offerings must be made, and this is something Isese, Santeria, Haitian Voodoo, and Hoodoo have in common.

The offering can be a lit candle, food, drink, or a special item. The honoring ceremony might not be as loud as Santeria or Haitian Voodoo, but it is rich with deep feelings and emotions. Usually, Hoodooists ask the ancestors to take away illnesses or challenges that have been affecting their lives.

Hoodoos deeply connect with their ancestors because of their high communication level. Practitioners practice spiritual readings with their ancestors. They may get a yes, no, or maybe through a spiritual medium. Practitioners use corn shells, tarot cards, and other tools to understand what the spirits say.

They leave an animal sacrifice or a fruit basket next to a tree in the name of their ancestors. The tree should be close to the person's house and is yet another way of respecting and showing appreciation to the spirits.

Like Santeria, some practitioners sing to their ancestors. However, the songs are sung by one individual, usually during their private time with their ancestors. Practitioners light candles for the spirits and must energetically cleanse the space before and after a prayer, or a ceremony is conducted.

Honoring the ancestors is a sacred activity shared by many African Spiritual beliefs. No matter how different they are from one another, remembering the spirits is a divine practice conducted yearly or daily.

African spirituality revolves around the connection between the individual, nature, and spirits. This connection must be kept even when the living takes a different form. Therefore, it is essential that practitioners continue honoring the dead, so their connection remains strong and alive. The spirits are seen as deities who have wisdom and power. They are believed to influence your life for the better, so practitioners ask for their guidance and help.

African spiritual practices like Santeria and Isese do not see ancestors as only relatives. The ancestors can be anyone linked to the religion or the practitioner's history. On the other hand, Haitian Voodoo sees the ancestors as relatives or close friends. Isese is similar to Haitian Voodoo since it also defines ancestors by bloodline or their relationship to the practitioner.

Offerings are a common element between these beliefs. When people honor their spirits through offerings, it is seen as a way to welcome their ancestors, honor them, and show them respect. The tools used during the ceremony differ from one belief to the other. However, it does not matter what tools you use so long as your heart is in the right place when honoring your loved ones.

Whether you were born into African spiritual traditions through ancestral roots or an outsider with a deep sense of belonging, you must respect the faith's beliefs and adhere to its rules. The consequences of disrespect and arrogance will significantly impact your life negatively. These traditions have survived for centuries due to the followers' devout faith.

Chapter 7: Sacred Herbs and Plants

Herbalism is sacred knowledge, and African spiritualists are no strangers to it. Whether the root, stem, petals, or leaves, nearly every part of the plant is used in all spellwork. This chapter explains the different herbs heavily used by African practitioners. If you have been trying to find herbs for love or protection spells, you'll find them in this chapter. Other herbs are also explained to help with power, prosperity, purification, spirits, and lust.

Certain herbs and plants are considered to be sacred.
https://unsplash.com/photos/7LsyosoO0GQ

It is common to ingest certain herbs during ceremonies and spellwork. However, you must be careful what you are ingesting. For starters, it is probably best to avoid ingesting any herb or plant if you are a beginner spellcaster. If you do not know whether you are allergic to certain herbs or plants, you should avoid swallowing anything. You can always burn the herb instead of consuming it and see its power manifest.

Adam and Eve Root

The Adam and Eve root is mainly used for love spells. Its spiritual properties are associated with matters of love, connection, and lust. Practitioners anoint the root with attraction essential oils, like clary sage, lavender, jasmine, or rose.

This root is used on same-sex couples and opposite-sex couples. The Adam and Eve root can be worn as an amulet carried by the couple or anointed daily to strengthen the love and spice up the relationship.

Agrimony

Agrimony is a versatile herb. It is mainly used for protection purposes but also to remove energy blockages. This herb is typically used in protection spells and is the main ingredient practitioners use to break jinxes.

People practicing Hoodoo magic use agrimony to clear energetic blockages. They also use it to cleanse their tools before working on their spells. Burning agrimony is common for protecting themselves against the evil eye. Often, spiritualists use this herb as candle dressing when working on a spell that breaks gossip or stops people from badmouthing them. It is common for people to burn agrimony to strengthen their energetic field.

Basil

Basil is commonly used in all African witchcraft. It is associated with prosperity, luck, and happiness. Practitioners use it to invite prosperity into their lives and bring in more money. They anoint a green candle with dried basil leaves and cast a spell allowing money to flow smoothly toward them. Some people carry basil with them when gambling because it is seen as a lucky charm.

Other practitioners use basil as a healing herb. Besides curing and warding off illnesses, it also energizes the spellcaster since it helps with fatigue and brain fog. Female practitioners dress a red candle with basil oil to relieve painful menstruation.

Bay Leaves

Spiritualists from different backgrounds use this herb because of its high versatility. Some use it to draw in money, and others to cast against evil eyes, banish harmful spells, and release themselves from work and family problems. The outcome of this herb depends on the spell and how you use it.

It is common in African spirituality to wash with bay leaf water. It is believed that washing hands and feet with this water increases the chances of receiving money. Other practitioners save bay leaf water to cleanse their doors and mirrors. Why? Because it brings positive energy and gets rid of negativity entering the house.

Belladonna

Belladonna is an herb that must be used with caution. **It should not be ingested or inhaled in any way.** This herb is associated with hallucination, seduction, and magic. It is usually used in love spells and on voodoo dolls.

Beginner practitioners are advised against using it because of its power, and it is tricky to work with when you do not have enough experience with witchcraft.

Some voodooists stuff belladonna into voodoo dolls when working on a love spell. Usually, this spell involves increasing a person's allure to seduce them. Others merely carve the individual's name onto a red candle and anoint it with belladonna to attract them toward themselves.

Cedar

Cedar smoke is famous for sharpening psychic abilities and hearing from spirits. It is also known for its rejuvenation capabilities. Spiritualists use cedar to feel energized and heal from aching or tired bodies. Cedar is used for warding off illnesses, so it is common to be around cedar smoke when a spiritualist feels they are about to get sick.

Voodooists use cedar smoke to sanctify their voodoo dolls. This sanctification ritual is the last part of a voodoo doll creation. The cedar blesses the doll and protects it from any unwanted energies.

Cedar smoke is used to sharpen psychic abilities and ward off illness.
https://unsplash.com/photos/zI84PsYBODg

Chamomile

Chamomile is another highly versatile herb. Some practitioners use it to ensure their manifestations come true, while others use it to have better dreams.

African practitioners put chamomile in their Mojo bags to increase their winning chances in gambling. Others fill their sachets with chamomile and put them under their pillows to have better dreams and decrease their chances of experiencing nightmares and sleep paralysis.

Some spiritualists bathe with chamomile water to increase allure and self-love. Others sprinkle dried chamomile petals around the house to ward off negative energies and entities from their space.

Cinnamon

Cinnamon is a powerful plant associated with financial prosperity and protection. If you want to invite money into your life, follow this spell.

On the first of every month, put some cinnamon powder in your hands and blow it onto your front door. You can do the same with your shop, company, etc. When you are blowing the cinnamon powder, visualize yourself receiving money and feel the emotions you would experience with prosperity. After you blow the powder, rub it into your hands. Washing it away may lessen the intensity of the spell.

When working on a protection spell, anoint a piece of paper with your name on it with cinnamon, or dress a white candle in cinnamon and picture yourself being shielded from negativity and people who wish you harm.

John the Conqueror Root

This root is highly valuable among Hoodoos. According to folklore, John the conqueror fell in love with Lilith, the devil's daughter. The devil challenged John and promised him Lilith's hand should he successfully complete the challenges. John bravely took on the challenges, but he knew the devil would kill him. Knowing this, John and Lilith stole the devil's horse and escaped to Africa. They agreed never to use their powers again so they could not be found and murdered by Lilith's father. John put his powers into the root in the United States and escaped with Lilith.

Today, Hoodoos use this root to be blessed by John's power. Practitioners dress white candles with this root seeking protection and peace. Others anoint red and pink candles with this root to attract love. People use this root with green candles to receive money and increase their luck.

Hyssop

Hyssop is a popular herb in African witchcraft. It is mainly used in purification and cleansing rituals. It is common for practitioners to bathe in its water before and after working on a powerful spell.

Haitian Voodooists sprinkle its water on their altars, while the Hoodoos clean their mojo bags and gris-gris with the herb's smoke. Others like to clean their witchcraft tools with hyssop water or smoke before spellcasting. The tools must be purified from previous spells. Otherwise, the consequences could be dire. Spiritualists also put Hyssop's purple flowers and leaves in their mojo bags to protect themselves from evil deities and entities.

Jimson Weed

The Jimson weed was used among Voodooists during slavery. They believed this herb eased the possession process. During the ceremonies, the individual consumed this herb and would be possessed by a spirit or an ancestor.

To this day, this herb should not be consumed without supervision. Multiple witnesses have claimed the herb causes people to have a complete lack of self-awareness. Researchers, Busia and Heckles, noted that the herb causes a "bodily frenzy" during possession ceremonies.

Voodooists use this herb to reach refined consciousness levels. Not everyone feels safe taking this root, so it is best not to consume it if you are not experienced with it or are not surrounded by professionals who can ensure your safety.

Lavender

This flower has various spiritual properties, like attracting love, and beauty, increasing money, and enhancing intuition. The flower's purple hues are associated with intuition and psychic abilities. Mixing lavender with rose petals is known to draw love into a person's life and enhance their physical allure. Carrying lavender around makes the person financially richer.

If you want to partake in any of these spells, pay close attention to these instructions:

- To increase your allure and find love, draw a bath, sprinkle it with lavender and rose petals, and soak your body in the water. If you do not have a bathtub, put lavender and rose petals in a sachet and hang the sachet over the shower head. Let the water run through and shower with its water.

- If you want more money, put lavender in a green sachet with a few coins. Carry this sachet on you, especially if you are on your way to work or to gamble.

- To strengthen your intuition, burn some lavender and surround yourself with its smoke. Exercise your intuition by praying to the ancestors or practicing your psychic abilities during this time. The lavender will sharpen your intuition to achieve better results.

Lucky Hand Root

From the name, you can gather that this root's spiritual properties are related to luck. The lucky hand root is an excellent herb to have on you when competing, gambling, or taking part in the lottery.

You can wear this herb, keeping it close to your chest, or put it in your mojo bag. Many Hoodoos replace their mojo bag with a lucky hand root because it is that powerful. People who carry this root, instead of a mojo bag, usually anoint the lucky hand with essentials, like cinnamon and sandalwood, to enhance their luck and ensure their winnings.

Mandrake Root

The mandrake root is close to the Voodoo dolls' function. In other words, it can heal or harm someone. For instance, let's say you created a Voodoo doll to heal a client. Instead of creating a Voodoo doll from scratch, you can carve the client's name into the root and proceed with your healing ceremony.

This root is incredibly powerful, especially if you manifest something in your life. For example, carve your name into the root and apply herbs and oils associated with success and prosperity if you want to manifest success and wealth.

If you use this root, you must be careful with its location and ingesting it. This root can heavily influence someone's life, so you must ensure you are the only person with access to it. Also, avoid ingesting the root since it is not meant for human consumption.

Maguey Root

Santeros, Santeria priests, believe the maguey root has incredible healing powers. It is highly common to drink maguey root tea if you practice Santeria since they believe it heals illnesses and wards off negativity. Hoodoos use this root as a charm that boosts the mojo bag's power. This root is used with red candles to increase lust in a relationship or make someone fall in love with you. Maguey root is used to spiritually cleanse the self from negative spirits and energies.

p

Rattlesnake Root

Burning rattlesnake root with the intention of attracting love brings the right people into your life and protects you from individuals not meant for you.

Spiritualists say that this root may make people leave your life, but, in reality, the root shields you from people who are not right for you. If you have a love interest and want to know whether they are a good fit, then you use this root. However, if you do not want to experience the harsh reality the root might expose you to, then maybe this is not the time to use it.

Rue

If you think someone has cast a spell on you or has hexed you, you might need to bathe with rue water. Practitioners sprinkle rue in their bathtubs to break hexes and jinxes.

Other practitioners prefer to drink rue tea instead of bathing in it, but again, it is better not to drink any herb if you do not know what effect it will have on your body.

Spiritualists believe sprinkling rue leaves outside their houses can bring them prosperity and luck. If you want more wealth in your life, you are more likely to attract prosperity if you blow cinnamon onto your door and sprinkle rue leaves outside of it.

Sage

Sage is another herb all African practitioners use. It is mainly known for its cleansing properties. For instance, Yoruba people and Hoodoos use sage smoke to cleanse their altars.

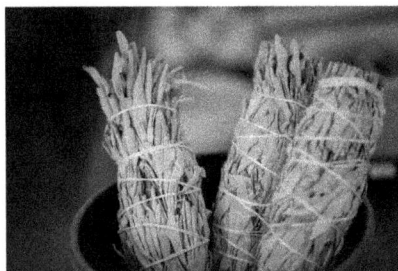

Sage is used to cleanse.
https://unsplash.com/photos/k44X7D5bpms

Haitian Voodooists use sage to cleanse themselves and their house. For example, let's say you had a guest in your house, and after they left, you felt the house's energy took a turn for the worst. In this scenario, the best thing to do is grab a sage bundle or sage leaves and burn them. Open a window so that the negative energy has a place to go, away from your house. Your house's energy will be replenished and renewed.

Sampson Snake Root

The Sampson snake root enhances male fertility and sexual performance. It is also used to gain power and respect in the community or workplace.

Practitioners usually soak the herb with whiskey and consume 1 tablespoon every day. Others prefer to make it into tea and drink it. Male practitioners wanting to perform better sexually wash their genitals with its water to get the full effect of this powerful root.

People who want to increase their male energy use this root. In other words, women can use this root, too. As people, we all have feminine and male energies, so people who want to connect with their male energies will benefit from using the Sampson Snake Root.

Saw Palmetto Berry

The Saw Palmetto Berry is mainly used by people practicing Santeria. People mix it with their alcohol and use it as an aphrodisiac. It is considered one of the main ingredients in love and lust spells. Practitioners also add honey to it to enhance its love-inducing powers.

During sex magic ceremonies, the saw palmetto berry is soaked with liquor and served to the participants. The drink prepares them for the energies and emotions they are about to experience.

Other practitioners use the berries as love charms and put them in their mojo bags or around the Voodoo doll to increase love and lust.

Sassafras

Sometimes practitioners find themselves targeted by other spellcasters. These practitioners could be victims of bad hexes or harmful entities. One way they protect themselves is by stuffing a mojo bag with sassafras leaves and leaving it near their bed or under their pillow.

The sassafras leaves are known for their protective properties. They mainly shield from evil entities and hexes or harmful spells. However, the sassafras leaves must be replaced with new ones every 2 days, depending on the entity you are dealing with. Change the mojo bag every 2 days to ensure your safety.

Solomon Seal Root

This root binds spirits, good and evil. Some practitioners use it to call on good spirits to protect themselves against evil entities targeting them. Others call on the spirits to get ahead in life or seek revenge on people who have wronged them.

Working with this root can be tricky and challenging. Novice practitioners are advised to avoid this root because it needs a lot of energy and experience they do not have. So, if you are not an advanced spellcaster, work with easier roots before using the Solomon seal root.

Quita Maldicion

The Quita Maldicion is a popular herb in Santeria. This plant is mostly known as the "curse remover" within the community. If you or someone you love is exhibiting symptoms of being cursed, it is best to burn quita maldicion around them. This herb also comes in handy when removing a hex or the evil eye from yourself or someone else. Remember, burning this herb removes curses, but they do not prevent them. So, the next time you are cleansing yourself from an evil eye or a curse, make sure to use herbs that also shield you from them. Moreover, do not use both herbs together. First, remove the curse, cleanse yourself with sage, and lastly, burn an herb to shield you from future harm.

Frescura Herb

The frescura herb is excellent for curing energy blockings. If you feel your house has lost its energy or has weird energy, then you need to burn this plant. You can also use it if your energy is blocked. How can you tell if your energy is blocked? Your intuition will not be as sharp, you may feel tired, and, most importantly, your spark will gradually fade away. Energy blockings are temporary, so you do not need to worry. Burn this plant to restore your energy and have it run smoothly through your body.

There are a plethora of herbs and plants to use on candles or bathe with. Moreover, other spells require ingesting certain plants but avoiding consuming any plant or root is best. However, if you are sure you will not suffer from a bad reaction, it is safe to ingest these ingredients. But, if you are unsure or have not consumed certain herbs before, it is best to avoid ingesting them. You can take allergy tests and always ask a health professional about the plants and roots you are curious about. Remember, not every spell here is for beginners, so if you are a novice, work with easier ingredients and spells that match your level. It is better to gain experience before working on challenging spells. Good luck, and be safe.

Chapter 8: Let's Talk about Altars and Shrines

Altars and shrines are considered highly delicate topics, as most African spiritual traditions require initiation. Therefore, you should always seek a priest's guidance and approval before you build your shrine and use it to work with your ancestors or the Orishas.

Altars and shrines are sacred in African spirituality practices.
Ji-Elle, CC BY-SA 4.0 <https://creativecommons.org/licenses/by-sa/4.0>, via Wikimedia Commons https://commons.wikimedia.org/wiki/File:La_Havane-Vente_d%27articles_religieux-Santer%C3%ADDa_(4).jpg

At-home shrines and altars are relatively easy to set up. They're great because they can be adapted to a wide range of beliefs and faiths. A sacred spot for spiritual practices, rituals, and prayers helps strengthen your connection with the deities and the spirits and replenishes your faith. Regardless of your belief system, an altar can help you recharge and maintain your peace and inner comfort.

On reading this chapter, you'll understand the structure and general layout of altars in Yoruba, Santeria, Hoodoo, and Haitian Vodou. You learn about their differences and similarities and discover how each spiritual tradition sets up and works with Orisha and ancestor altars. Finally, we give you tips on how to build your own at-home altar.

Yoruba

Yoruba altars come in various sizes and appearances. A shrine's exact form differs from one practitioner's preferences and ideologies to the other. Yoruba shrines aren't typically ornate and humungous, and the best thing about them is they could be adapted to the space, monetary, and tool limitations of the average person. They are much like the characteristics the saint withholds.

Yorubas use shrines to communicate with the saints, so they're typically located on a higher level than the ground. A Yoruba altar is a sacred space where you can make offerings, perform sacrifices, pray, or partake in other spiritual activities. Your choice of practices and offerings mainly depends on whether you dedicate your altar to Orishas or ancestors. There's no need to worry if you want to worship Orishas and ancestors simultaneously because the Yoruba religion doesn't require altars to be immovable once set up.

On specific days of the year, such as October 4th and December 17th, Orula and San Lazaro days, respectively, practitioners build great altars and celebrate together. People also dedicate a large portion of their homes to making colorful altars with numerous symbols, representatives, and offerings.

Christian Yorubas often incorporate Catholic saints into their shrines. Most commonly include the Virgin of Rule, the Virgin of the Mercedes, Saint Barbara, and the Charity of the Copper, among other significant figures. They further decorate the shrines with fruits, candles, and flowers. The Yoruba Orishas are represented with ceramic, guira, porcelain, or clay soup containers in order of hierarchy.

Figures of the deities are placed on stones in the soup bowls and are typically adorned with rings, robes, and other symbols associated with the Orishas and the saints. These typically include food, drinks, flowers, fruit offerings, fans, toys, and tools. What you do to work with or honor an Orisha depends on its unique preferences and characteristics.

When preparing an ancestor shrine, you must seek a priest's help because you need to obtain 9 sticks from a specific tree and ritually prepare them before tying them together using a red cloth. This bundle of sticks is what you'll be making your offerings to. You also need an "Opa egun," any thick, straight, and tall wooden branch for your invocations. A male practitioner will use it to tap on the floor as you, or someone else, invoke the ancestors. Always offer them the first serving of any meal. Water or liquor is also typically offered.

Santeria

Like Yoruba, many major Orishas in Santeria have Catholic counterparts. You can build a shrine to honor the Orisha you wish to worship and honor using symbols and colors that represent them and make relevant offerings.

Yorubas and Santeria practitioners share the same belief regarding ancestors; they pass onto the invisible world to watch over their loved ones. However, only those who qualified to be honored through ancestor work can live up to their destiny. These are often people who lived honorable lives and contributed to their society. Those people should have also experienced long lives and natural deaths.

Some people dedicate a separate space or even a separate building for their altars. It depends on family traditions and personal preferences. Ancestor altars commonly include a white candle and cloth. Pictures or belongings of the ancestor, flowers, or three water glasses (you can use any odd number of water glasses) should also be added. Some people like to separate the male and female ancestors on the altar. Some people also separate different families, which would be a great idea for individuals who never get along well.

If you're setting up an Orisha altar., keep all the Orishas (except for the warrior deities) in ceramic tureens. The color and decoration of the tureen depend on the characteristics and symbols of the Orisha you're working with. These tureens hold the sacred stones of the Orishas, which is an extension of the Yoruba tradition of placing stones in bowls or pots.

If you're working with a warrior Orisha, avoid using tureens. Keep them in uncovered iron or clay pots. Use sealed containers with water for the water Orishas. Each Orisha accepts unique offerings, often left beside their tureen or another vessel. Some offerings, known as ebó, are considered sacrifices because they are either purchased, which is a financial sacrifice, or made, which is a sacrifice of time. Making a weekly ebó for the Orisha can keep it strong and pleased.

Hoodoo

Hoodoo practitioners prepare their altar by visiting their ancestors' graves with a small container. They introduce themselves and notify the ancestors of their intentions. They store a little dirt in the container, take it home, and use it to build a connection with the ancestor.

Hoodoo practitioners spoon the dirt into their containers by digging with coins near their ancestor's graves after pouring whiskey over the grave. When they get home, they empty the dirt into a nicer-looking container.

According to Hoodoo traditions, Saturday is ideal for working with the dead. They usually make food offerings of meat and potatoes and some dyed pale blue water. They set up a basic altar for their ancestors and create them weekly with music, food, or other offerings. You can also serve your ancestor's favorite dishes.

You can include several containers with grave dirt from different people's altars, with their pictures and a few of their belongings. Some practitioners include an empty picture frame as a symbol of the relatives and ancestors they don't know.

Haitian Vodou

Haitian Vodou shrines are known for their vibrant colors and magnificence. The Orishas are typically represented in their own spots. Haitian Vodou shrines incorporate several objects required by the deities, or Lwa, depending on who you're working with. Other tools, like decorated bottles, are considered offerings and serve a specific purpose.

Filled and empty bottles are usually ornamented with images and specific symbols. They are often covered with sequins or other colorful decorations. While dolls are used, they're not as terrifying as Voodoo dolls are thought to be. Many people believe practitioners stick pins in these dolls to cast harmful curses on others. However, they are used to honor certain deities. Some people employ dolls as messengers between the physical realm and the spirits. Herb-filled cloth packets are also popular altar decorations. The colors of the pieces of cloth and how they're decorated depend on the colors of the Lwas. These packets are believed to bring protection and stimulate healing. Interestingly, Haitian Vodou practitioners leave flags leaning against an altar as ritual objects that attract the Lwa to replenish its spiritual energy.

Building Your Altar

Decide Its Purpose

The first thing you must do before building your altar is to determine its purpose. Which spiritual path are you following? Do you intend to build an Orisha or ancestor altar? Do you have a specific deity you wish to honor? Will you use your altar for celebrations? Is your altar movable, or must it be fixed?

You need to ensure your altar offers a comfortable space, as you could use it to meditate, pray, communicate with your ancestors, make invocations, or conduct other rituals.

Decide Where to Place It

The location and size of your altar mainly depend on your needs, lifestyle, and preferences. Some people like to dedicate an entire room to their spiritual practices, while others believe their dresser or bookshelf would suffice. However, when setting up your altar, it should face a meaningful or pleasant direction. For instance, if you're building an ancestor altar, face it toward the direction of your ancestor's homeland.

It's best if you build your altar somewhere quiet and private. This way, you won't have to worry about someone knocking it over or interrupting your spiritual practices. You don't need to rush to find the right location. Some people are drawn toward a spot that just "feels right." Consider the energy this place gives off. Is it welcoming and bright? You can use smudging or other energy-cleansing techniques before you set up your space. It also helps if you do an energetic cleanse every once in a while.

Find Out Which Tools You Need

Even though there are some rules you must follow when setting up your altar, especially if you're working with specific Orishas, you'll often have to lean into your intuition. Pay attention to your cravings and signs to pick up on the offerings the Orishas wish to receive. Your gut may also signal certain objects to incorporate into your ancestor shrine. Unless you're going against instructions, there are no limits to what you're allowed to keep on your altar. However, always ask for your priest's opinion until you've gained enough confidence in your own knowledge.

Candles are very popular tools to add to your altar and are often required when working with certain Orishas. Be careful not to leave your burning candles unattended, and keep them away from flammable materials. Be extra careful if you have any children or pets at home.

Set Up Your Altar

Once you've cleaned your space energetically, think about how you'd like to arrange your tools and objects on your altar. Start with a few items to avoid feeling overwhelmed. As a rule of thumb, keep your altar symmetrical, with the tallest item in the middle. Cover your table or surface with a cloth if you wish to protect it from candle wax, ash, or other potentially damaging objects.

Maintain Your Efforts

You should aim to use your altar habitually. If it's too much pressure, start with a seasonal practice and build from there. For instance, if you practice Yoruba, set up an altar to commemorate notable celebrations. Once you feel ready, you can build an Orisha or ancestor altar and tend to it once a week. If working with an altar becomes a habit, you can easily incorporate it into your daily routine.

Your day will eventually feel incomplete without the 10 or 15 minutes you spend at your altar daily.

Most importantly, your altar must always be clean and organized, no matter how often you use it. You should exude positive emotions each time you approach your altar; it should never feel like a chore. If you beat yourself up for not praying today, you'll eventually dread having to do it. Instead of being a peaceful space you can retreat in, it will feel heavy and suffocating. Refurbish your altar, remove items you no longer need, and introduce new ones every now and then. Clean the altar and everything on it often.

Your altar or shrine must be in a place where you won't be interrupted. You should dedicate the time to connecting with your ancestors for peace and guidance. Know your purpose for contacting them – have your questions prepared beforehand.

Now that you have read this chapter, you understand how different African spiritual traditions use altars and shrines. You are ready to build your ancestor or Orisha's altar with the guidance of an experienced priest. These spiritual traditions have been used for centuries, so they will work for you if you believe in the system.

Chapter 9: Mojo Bags and Gris-Gris

Mojo bags and gris-gris are typically mistaken as the same. However, both tools have significant differences. You must learn the distinctions between both instruments to guarantee a safe practice environment and experience.

This chapter delves deep into the differences between these talismans to identify the right one for you. You'll learn how mojo bags and gris-gris are created and how they're cleansed, consecrated, charged, stored, and safely used.

Mojo bag.

Teogomez, CC BY-SA 3.0 <http://creativecommons.org/licenses/by-sa/3.0/>, via Wikimedia Commons https://commons.wikimedia.org/wiki/File:Grisgristuareg.JPG

The History of Mojo Bags

Mojo bags were brought to America by enslaved Africans centuries ago. Making these mojo bags and carrying them around in their pockets was the only thing that kept them sane as they endured the terrors of the slave trade. Mojo bags were a lot more than talismans to enslaved Africans. They were a means of assurance and offered a sense of security in a highly cruel and uncertain environment. Soon, these small, good-luck charms were incorporated into Hoodoo, a traditional magical system.

The incredible thing about mojo bags and the entire practice of Hoodoo is they combine many African, Native American, and even European magical practices and traditions. Some people believe these talismans have a great number of similarities with medicine bags, which are indigenous to the Native Americans. Both magical tools incorporate several personal and natural items to induce a specific, powerful effect, and both are carried discreetly or kept in a safe place.

Mojo Bags

Mojo bags are created to attract certain things and energies into a person's life. Various mojo bags serve a wide array of purposes. For instance, you can create one to attract protection into your life and another to initiate love. Mojo bags come in different colors, depending on the energy and the results you wish to achieve.

A mojo bag contains various stones, herbs, and other trinkets that can help you manifest your desires. You must set a clear intention, name your mojo bag, and replenish it every now and then. A mojo bag must first be slept with to set its effects in motion. Keeping it under your pillow or bed or placing it beside you as you sleep allows you to bond with it. The main objective behind this practice is to amalgamate its essence with yours. Wear your mojo bag or keep it on you, but it should never be visible to others.

This talisman can transform or elevate several areas of your life. It can make you more successful, keep you in good health, protect you from potential harm, attract love and abundance into your life, and more. Think of it as an amulet charged with spells and magic. Many people regard mojo bags as mystical beings you must feed and properly care for, as it is the only way they will grow their powers and redirect their energies into their holders' lives.

Making and Using a Mojo Bag

Choose a cloth bag that aligns with your desire and intention. These pouches come in a wide array of colors and fabrics and are available at any craft store. Use the following list as a guide to help you choose the color that corresponds with your intention:

- Orange: success, stamina, endurance, and vitality.

- Purple: divination and spirituality. It's also used when overcoming and healing from karmic lessons.

- Red: protection, courage, and passion. Red could also be associated with marriage.

- Blue: wisdom and philosophy. Blue is considered the color of intellect.

- Black: protection and eliminating negativity. It is also related to discipline.

- Yellow: self-expression, happiness, and creativity.

- Pink: love, romance, and friendship. Pink also corresponds with art, emotional healing, and beauty.

- Grey: secrets and mysteries. It also represents neutrality.

- Green: wealth, abundance, and prosperity. Green is also associated with luck and employment.

- Silver: receptivity and meditation.

- White: peace and psychological healing. White is considered the color of angelic guidance.

- Gold: projectivity and prosperity.

After choosing a color that corresponds with what you want to manifest, you need to fill it with relevant symbols, herbs, and stones. While the possibilities are endless, here's a small list of items that correspond to certain purposes to get you started:

- Wealth: pyrite, emerald, bayberry, coins, and cinnamon

- Victory: nasturtium, High John the conqueror root, and carnelian

- Love: catnip, honey, rose, rose quartz, almond, and morganite
- Health: lobelia, hematite, clove, bloodstone, and orange peel
- Protection: salt, borage, black tourmaline, basil, morning glory

Consider hand-sewing your mojo bag instead of purchasing a ready-made one, as this helps amplify its effects. Here's how to do it:

1. Measure the width of your ribbon, and cut it at length 3 times as long. For instance, if you're using a 2-inch-wide ribbon, make it 6 inches long.

2. Fold it in half, ensuring both halves are perfectly aligned.

3. Sew the sides together, leaving around 1.25 inches unsewn at the end. The top must not be sewn, as this will be the mojo bag's opening.

4. Turn the ribbon inside out, hiding the stitching inside.

5. Fold the 1.25-inch flaps outside and down and make around 4 small cuts along both folds.

6. Unfold the flaps and thread a string through the cuts around the bag's circumference.

7. Fill your bag with your selected items and firmly tie the drawstrings into a knot.

8. To feed your mojo bag, anoint it with an essential oil or burn incense and pass it through the smoke. You should set a clear intention as you do this.

Keep the mojo bag in your pocket or underneath your pillow. If you feel comfortable with where you keep it, let it stay there. If not, try different locations until you find one that feels right. You should recharge your mojo bag regularly by feeding it. Most people do recharge it every full moon.

Gris-Gris

Many confuse mojo bags with gris-gris because the latter also serves as a talisman in a small satchel. However, the primary purpose of a gris-gris is to protect its holder from the evil eye and unwanted energies. The catch is that you must incorporate a body part of yours, or whoever wishes protection, into the satchel. This is how the holder connects with the gris-gris and becomes one with its essence.

Besides grisly ingredients like bones, hairs, and nails, this talisman also includes crystals, herbs, and other magical tools and ingredients. Unlike mojo bags, gris-gris is considered to be associated with black magic and darker arts.

A gris-gris creates a potent dark shield around its holder to keep negative and unwanted energy away. The talisman achieves this effect because it has to encounter heavier and darker magic at first.

Gris-gris is a Voodoo practice that can get very dangerous if not used mindfully. You need to be very careful with your intentions and what you're asking of this talisman. Also, you must put a lot of thought into the ingredients you use to make your gris-gris. Adding your body part can significantly amplify your connection with the talisman. Novices and anyone not ready for this bond won't handle its intensity and effects.

Making and Using a Gris-Gris

When creating a gris-gris, be very mindful of what you think and feel. You should only make or use a gris-gris whenever you're experiencing a positive state of mind. Direct all your attention with love and positivity toward your intention, whether you're making it for yourself or someone else. Be as specific as possible when expressing and wording your intention. Have unwavering faith in the talisman's ability to protect you from potential harm.

It's best to use a black pouch, as this is the color of protection and the banishing of negative energy. Also, use protective symbols, crystals, and herbs, such as salt, borage, black tourmaline, and basil. However, when creating a gris-gris, allow your instincts to take the lead.

You can include your desired number of items in the gris-gris as long as you end up with an odd number. Keep the number of items between 3 and 13, including your lock of hair or fingernail and the shells and charms. If you're making the gris-gris for someone else, ask them to add their hair or fingernails to the bag.

Cleanse and purify your space before you start making the gris-gris. If you have an altar, use it as a workstation. If not, find a place you typically associate with healing and positive energies. For example, dining tables are ideal because this is where warm family gatherings take place.

Wipe your surface clean and burn incense or sage. Many people prefer burning juniper leaves. When you're done, use cedar sticks to smudge the space or sweep the negative energy away with a ceremonial or old wooden broomstick. You don't need to sweep the floor. Just circle your broom around it. Lay your ingredients in front of you and light a candle in the center of your table. Say, "Bless this space and all power brought forth," as you light the candle. Ask for the universe's guidance and call upon a deity, an ancestor, spirit guides, or any higher power you wish to work with. Ask them to guide you throughout this endeavor.

If you're making a gris-gris for someone else, keep their picture in front of you or carve their name into the candle you use. Insert each item into the bag, thanking the stone, flower, or tree in the process. Be fully present and hold onto your intention throughout the process. Speak your desire for protection out loud. Once you tie your bag, thank the universe, your higher powers, and Mother Nature for their help, and then blow out the candle.

Recite your intention every night throughout the duration of each waning moon and until the new moon arrives.

Whenever you're creating a gris-gris, remember whatever thoughts, emotions, or intentions you send out to the universe will come back to you threefold. Therefore, always express your gratitude and be positive while creating the bag. If you're creating a gris-gris for someone else, ask their permission first. Avoid using gris-gris to influence other people's wills, and be very specific and mindful of your intentions.

Which Talisman Should I Go For?

If you're open to experimenting with different energies and magic, you probably feel conflicted about which talisman to use. Mojo bags are generally more versatile, which is why many people prefer using them. They can be adapted to your personal goals, intentions, and needs. Anyone who feels more comfortable using white or red magic spells should go for mojo bags.

Gris-gris is interesting to use. Some people enjoy the extra thought (and added risk) of creating and using this talisman. However, they're quite challenging and require a degree of knowledge and experience with black magic.

Mojo bags are great because they can be approached from a positive standpoint. When you feed it positive energy, expect it to send it back. Since mojo bags apply to a plethora of magic, they should be approached with love and an airy feel, which is very important in protecting yourself from negative energies surrounding you.

Some people don't feel comfortable incorporating parts of their bodies into magical practices. Your opinion regarding this matter makes you neither less nor more qualified to use talismans. It merely helps you determine which magic to use. Practitioners of dark arts lean toward using gris-gris, while green witches (they rely on essential oils, roots, herbs, and other natural ingredients) feel more at ease when using gris-gris.

If you're new to the world of magic or African spirituality, it could take some time to discover your scope and the areas you enjoy working in. Take your time to experiment and explore your inclinations, as long as you do it safely and under proper guidance.

Each person is different, so remember you're free to set the horizon and limits for your unique practice. Once you feel more confident in your ability to use talismans, you'll discover there's no right or wrong way to this practice. You'll lean into your intuition to determine the practices that you resonate with.

Chapter 10: Festivals and Ceremonies

Festivals are important in many religions and spiritual traditions. They're a time when communities and families can come together. Furthermore, celebrating religious festivals is a time when adherents can publicly express their beliefs and strengthen their bond with their deities. Religious festivals and celebrations are also a time when communities can create and disseminate religious narratives and stories, which are then passed down through generations.

Festivals and ceremonies celebrate spirituality.
https://unsplash.com/photos/tGfB7t4L1JY

The importance of these festivals and ceremonies is evident in religions and spiritual practices around the world, and African spiritual practices and traditions are no different. Each religion and spiritual practice promotes and celebrates a different set of holidays, which have spiritual importance in the specific tradition.

Kemeticism and Kemetic Orthodoxy

Kemetic Orthodoxy is an offshoot of traditional Kemeticism (known as Egyptian paganism) and features many holidays celebrating Kemetic deities. Some major holidays in Kemetic Orthodoxy include:

Beautiful Feast of the Valley

Also known as the Feast of the Beautiful Valley, the Beautiful Feast of the Valley is an ancient Kemetic holiday that celebrates the dead. In the modern calendar, it is celebrated around April 28th.

This festival involves remembering the dead and those gone before and was the major festival in Thebes. It had grand processions to temples and tombs, where families would hold feasts with their ancestors. It was also a time to celebrate the god Amun, whose figure led these processions.

In the modern day, this festival often coincides with the pagan festival of Beltane and is celebrated similarly. It involves creating altars for the ancestors and eating meals with friends, family, and other loved ones.

Opet Festival

Also known as the Beautiful Feast of Opet, the Opet Festival was one of the most prominent ancient Kemetic holidays. The festival celebrated the deities Amun, Mut, and Khonsu and took place over 24 days. It was the most prominent celebration in Luxor.

The festival was celebrated during the flooding of the Nile. Therefore, it also acted as a festival and celebration of fertility. In the modern calendar, this festival is celebrated in June and celebrates the deities Amun, Mut, and Khonsu. While modern festival celebrations do not last 24 days, many adherents of Kemeticism leave the altars up throughout June and make daily offerings to replicate the ancient celebration.

Aset Luminous

Aset is another name for the Egyptian mother goddess Isis. It is a festival of lights and commemorates Aset's (Isis's) search for her brother-husband Wesir (Osiris) after their brother Set (Seth) traps and kills Osiris in a wooden coffin.

In the story, Aset searches for her husband everywhere, including at night, by the light of her torch. Kemetic adherents light candles, lamps, and torches to aid her in her search. Additionally, they create paper boats with prayers written on them and containing a light source (like a tealight candle) and place them on a water source (like a river) so that the goddess has light available wherever she goes.

This festival is generally in early July, around July 2nd.

Wep Ronpet

Wep Ronpet is essentially the Kemetic New Year. The date of this festival varies every year, but it is generally celebrated at the end of July or the beginning of August. The specific date depends on when the star Sirius rises at the Tawy temple (the primary temple of Kemetic Orthodoxy, based in Illinois, United States).

Wep Ronpet is preceded by 5 days known as Epagomenal Days. These days are celebrated as the birthdays of the four or five children of Geb and Nut – in order:

- Osiris
- Horus - in some traditions (particularly later Greco-Egyptian), there are two deities known as Horus – Horus the Elder is a child of Geb and Nut, and Horus the Younger is the child of Isis and Osiris
- Set
- Isis
- Nephthys

During the Epagomenal Days, care is taken not to take too many risks, as these days are considered outside the traditional year. On each day, worship is given to the relevant god's birthday, including creating shrines for each god and making offerings.

On the day of Wep Ronpet, adherents celebrate the New Year by clearing out the old – usually by cleaning their homes or places of work and celebrating the day with family and friends. For magic practitioners, the day could include renewing wardings, performing cleansings, and doing other protective work in and around the home.

Wag Festival

The Wag Festival, or Festival of the Wag, occurs in late August and commemorates and celebrates the god Wesir (Osiris). It was essentially a festival of the dead and a day to celebrate and remember the souls who passed before, especially in the year that had just passed.

Wag Festival is one of the oldest known Kemetic festivals and has been celebrated since the days of the Old Kingdom. In ancient Egypt, people celebrated the festival by creating small papyrus boats decorated with prayers and sending them out on the East bank of the Nile. It was a way to commemorate the death of Osiris.

Other celebrations included visiting their ancestors' tombs with offerings for the dead to keep them satisfied in the afterlife.

Today, people celebrate the festival by creating paper boats and sending them floating on local bodies of water. It is a day to create altars for the ancestors and to place your offerings.

Sed Festival

The Sed festival, or the Feast of the Tail, is an ancient Kemetic festival commemorating the continued rule of the pharaoh.

In modern times, this festival is celebrated to honor Horus the Younger, who acts as the king of the living. It is also a chance to honor the memories of the deceased Egyptian pharaohs. Other deities honored during the festival include Sekhmet and Wepwawet. The festival is held on November 15th in the modern calendar.

These are only a few festivals followed in Kemeticism and Kemetic Orthodoxy. Hundreds of festivals are celebrated in ancient Kemeticism (in some calendars, there is nearly one celebration for each day of the year). Modern followers often choose prominent holidays or holidays that celebrate their preferred deities to celebrate.

Isese

Known as the Yoruba religion, Isese is followed by the Yoruba people in Africa, particularly present-day Nigeria. Some Isese festivals include:

Eyo Festival

The Eyo festival is primarily celebrated in Lagos and is known as the Adamu Orisha Play. This festival is traditionally held to escort the spirit of a deceased king or chief and help welcome his successor. The festival pays homage to the ruling Oba (king or ruler) of Lagos.

The festival takes place over 24 days and involves a well-known parade featuring performers dressed in white robes. The festival gets its name from these costumed dancers called "Eyo."

This festival is held when required and often to honor and commemorate prominent members of the Lagos Yoruba community and its chiefs and kings. However, this festival is also held more frequently as a tourist event and is a well-known source of tourism in Lagos.

Osun-Osogbo Festival

The Osun-Osogbo festival is celebrated in August every year at the sacred Osun-Osogbo grove located along the banks of the Osun River outside Osogbo city.

This festival is a celebration of the Orisha Osun (Oshun), the Orisha of love, beauty, freshwater, and wealth. The festival is at least seven centuries old and is a two-week celebration that includes the following:

- A traditional cleansing of Osogbo
- The lighting of the 500-year-old, sixteen-point lamp, the Ina Olojumerindinlogun
- The Iboriade, where the crowns of previous Osogbo rulers are gathered and blessed
- A large procession in front of the Osun-Osogbo shrine. This procession is a celebration featuring dancing, musical performances, praise, poetry, costumed revelers, and more. The procession is led by the sitting ruler of Osogbo, the Ataoja, the Arugba (calabash carrier), and a group of priestesses.

This festival replicates the meeting between Osun and a group of migrants fleeing from famine. The Orisha agreed to provide them with prosperity in exchange for an annual sacrifice, and the festival includes this annual sacrifice.

Like the Eyo Festival, the Osun-Osogbo festival helps promote tourism to the local area, besides being followed for religious and spiritual reasons.

Sango Festival

The Sango festival dates to over 1000 years ago and is held in August. It is celebrated to honor and commemorate Sango, the Orisha of thunder and fire. Sango is also considered the founding father of the Oyo people and is believed to have been the third Alaafin of Oyo, making him an ancestor to the current royals.

This festival is celebrated in Oyo state in Nigeria, and the primary celebrations are generally held in the palace of the current Alaafin of Oyo.

It is a 10-day festival celebrated by followers dressed in red or white. Some celebrations include an ayo competition (one of the oldest Yoruba games played using a wooden board and pebbles), cultural and traditional displays, and magic performances. Like the Osun-Osogbo festival, the Sango festival is a public spectacle celebrated communally.

Igogo Festival

The Igogo festival is held annually, celebrated in September in Owo. This festival celebrates the Orisha Queen Oronsen. Oronsen was Olowo Rerengejen's wife.

This festival has been celebrated for at least 600 years and is a 17-day affair beginning with a procession of Iloro chiefs. The Olowo of Owo and the high chiefs of the kingdom dress like women. The Olowo also celebrates the festival of new yams at the same time, as it is incorporated into the Igogo festival. During the festival, guns are forbidden to be fired, drums should not be beaten, and using caps and head ties is prohibited.

Olojo Festival

The Olojo festival is celebrated annually in October in Ife, Osun state. The festival is celebrated in honor of Ogun, the Orisha of Iron, who is believed to be the eldest son of the progenitor of the Yoruba people, Oduduwa. The festival is also a celebration of the creation of the world.

For seven days before the festival, the Ooni of Ife must be secluded, offering prayers for his people and communing with the ancestors. On the day of the festival, he emerges from his seclusion, wearing the Aare crown, believed to be the original crown of Oduduwa.

Along with a crowd of adherents, the Ooni visits several sacred shrines to offer prayers and perform rituals. The shrines visited include the Okemogun shrine and shrines of historical importance. The rituals performed include ones that ask for peace in all Yoruba lands.

Oro Festival

The Oro festival is an annual festival that occurs across Yoruba land and is celebrated by all towns and settlements of Yoruba origin. It is a highly specific festival only celebrated by men who are descendants through their paternal ancestors, native to each location.

During the festival, women and descendants of non-natives must always stay indoors. People often travel to their native places to celebrate this festival.

As its name implies, the Oro festival celebrates the Orisha Oro, the Orisha of bullroarers and justice. It is believed that Oro should not be seen by women and non-natives, so they are expected to stay indoors during the festival. If anyone not meant to celebrate the festival ventures outside and catches a glimpse of Oro, they will die.

The festival lasts several days, and specific celebrations vary from settlement to settlement. Since the festival is so exclusive in its celebrants, very little is known about how it is actually celebrated.

Vodoun

Vodoun is a West African religion, known as Voudou and Voodoo, practiced by Aja, Ewe, and Fon peoples.

Fête du Vodoun

Fête du Vodoun is a festival celebrated annually on January 10th in Benin. The festival is a celebration of all things Vodoun, and celebrations start with the slaughter and sacrifice of a goat.

Followers dress as gods and perform rituals, and one of the best-known parts of the festival involves people dressing as Zangbeto (traditional Voodoo guardians) and performing. People also dress as Egungun, and spectators should avoid these individuals, as it is believed that if one of the Egungun touches you, you could die.

Other parts of the festival include singing, dancing, and drinking. Besides being extremely popular among Vodoun adherents, the festival is a well-known tourist attraction. Tourists travel from all over the world to be part of the celebration.

Haitian Voodoo

Haitian Voodoo shares some elements with Vodoun, but it is a different religion and features different celebrations.

Fête Gede

Known as the Haitian Day of the Dead and the Festival of the Ancestors, Fête Gede is celebrated annually on the first two days of November.

This festival involves a public procession, and many of the participants dress up. People commune with their ancestors and travel to graveyards to offer their ancestors food and drinks. The festival also celebrates the Iwa of death and fertility and involves music, dancing, and feasting.

However, before adherents can travel to their ancestors' graves, they must first honor and make offerings at the grave of Papa Gede, the first man to die. For people who cannot travel to Haiti for the festival, offerings are made at their altars first.

The Festival of the Miraculous Virgin of Saut d'Eau

The festival of the Miraculous Virgin of Saut d'Eau is less of a festival and more of a pilgrimage. It is held every year from July 14th to 16th. The Miraculous Virgin of Saut d'Eau, known as Saint Anne and Little Saint Anne, is considered the Virgin Mary's mother. She is believed to bring luck in romance and finance.

This festival is a pilgrimage to the Saut d'Eau waterfall, located north of Port-au-Prince. At the waterfall, Voodoo followers conduct purification rituals known as "luck baths." It involves bathing under the waterfall, after which a calabash (water flask made from a gourd) is broken. Additionally, the person leaves their clothes in the waterfall and wears new clothes, symbolizing the removal of past bad luck and introducing new good luck.

While this pilgrimage is primarily performed in July, it can be performed at any time of the year. The July pilgrimage also attracts numerous tourists interested in watching the pilgrimage.

Plaine Du Nord Festival

Known as the Plen Dino Festival, the Plaine Du Nord Festival occurs annually over two days in July and is celebrated in Plaine-du-Nord in northern Haiti.

This festival celebrates the Haitian Revolution, believed to have been aided by the deities and spirits. The festival also celebrates the Orisha Ogun, the Orisha of metal, soldiers, and blacksmiths.

During the festival, believers make offerings at the church of St. James or Ogoun Feraille. They offer prayers to the Virgin Mary of Mount Caramel, associated with Erzulie Freda, the goddess of love. Pilgrims offer sacrifices to the gods, including animals slaughtered as offerings.

Additionally, adherents take a ritual mud bath at St. Jacques's Hole, a sacred mud pool. These ritual baths are helped by priests who pray with pilgrims, and the baths act as a rebirth and baptism. The festival is also celebrated by limiting food and drink (not a complete fast), allowing pilgrims to experience the deprivations warriors during the Haitian Revolution experienced.

Conclusion

The African continent is home to some of the oldest civilizations in the world and has a rich history of spiritual practices. Learning about these spiritual practices is a great way to understand the people who practice them and can be a great stepping stone if you want to explore these practices as part of your spiritual journey.

As you've learned from this book, African spiritual practices are many and varied and include practices such as Haitian Vodou, Hoodoo, Santeria, and Kemetic Orthodoxy. While these traditions are unique and disparate, they also share some similarities, such as primarily oral traditions, ancestor worship, and a belief in the spirit world and supernatural beings like Santeria saints, Vodou Lwa, and Yoruba Orishas.

Many Africans believe in newer religions like Christianity and Islam. However, traditional religions and spiritual practices are once more growing in popularity. The growth of syncretic religions and traditions like Kemetic Orthodoxy reflects this interest in the history of African traditional religions, and this book is an introduction to these traditions.

To master any subject, you must first understand its history and fundamental concepts; African spiritual practices are no different. Once you've learned the basics of each tradition, you can find the one that speaks to you the most and explore them further.

Once you've learned about these traditions, it's also essential to learn about some of their practices – specifically, the importance of ancestor veneration, building altars and shrines, and using gris-gris and mojo bags. Ancestor veneration, in particular, is practiced by most traditional African spiritual practices and is a key pillar of the community on the continent.

Along with learning more about these practices, you should also focus on learning about the sacred herbs and plants of the African continent. These herbs and plants are key in many rituals and spells. They are often unfamiliar to non-African readers because of their traditional names or, in some cases, the difficulty of finding them outside Africa.

Similarly, it can be challenging to become familiar with many African spiritual practices because of unfamiliar terms and words. The glossary at the end of this book will help you, making it easier for you to understand the meaning of these words and how to pronounce them.

African spirituality is a rich, complex tapestry of traditions and practices often overlooked by the rest of the world. This book will help you understand the fundamentals of these beliefs and to get started on your journey to learning more about these fascinating traditions.

For many people, African spirituality is synonymous with evil and witchcraft. As you discovered from this book, this concept is far from the truth. These traditions are filled with deep emotions and rely on nature and gods.

Whether you're interested in this book as a guide to your spiritual journey or are merely looking to learn more about African spiritual practices, there's something in it for everyone. So, remember to keep this book by your side as you explore the world of African spirituality further. Good luck.

Glossary of Terms

African spiritual practices use plenty of foreign words and phrases that sound complicated and foreign to newcomers. While each term is thoroughly explained and discussed in the chapters, this chapter summarizes the difficult words used throughout the book. You can use it when looking up certain words while reading the book.

Commonly Used Terms in African Spiritual Practices

Ashe - the divine energy that can be obtained through African spiritual practices. Each Orisha has its distinct ache they offer for empowerment or blessing to devotees. Mentioned in chapter 1.

Akhu - known as akh, akhu are souls blessed after the death of their physical body because they survived this. These spirits emit a powerful (shining) energy, provide protection, and help find divine wisdom. Mentioned in chapter 2.

Ayo - is one of the oldest Yoruba games. It's played using a wooden board and pebbles during the Sango festival. Mentioned in chapter 10.

According to Kemetic Orthodox beliefs, Ba is the part of the soul that travels between the realms. Mentioned in chapter 2.

Baron Samedi - the most superior Lwa of the Ghede Lwa pantheon. He is the Lwa of death, and he greets the spirits of the dead and guides them on their journey to the other world. Mentioned in chapter 4.

Bondye - pronounced as "bohn-dyay,"- is a supreme being in Voodoo and Haitian Voodoo. He is the creator of the universe and the equivalent of Olodumare in the Yoruba religion. Mentioned in chapter 3.

Chango - known as Sango and Santa Barbara. Chango is the god of lightning and thunder, and he is associated with magic, masculinity, and sexuality. Mentioned in chapters 4 and 5.

Ebo - called ebbo. Ebo is a term used for offerings and sacrifices made to Orishas. Ebo can be presented in many forms, such as food, meals, objects, releasing live animals, etc. Mentioned in chapter 8.

Egun - these are the souls of deceased ancestors or spirits the practitioner feels close to. They are often blood relatives but can also be part of a person's religious family. Sometimes, spirit guides and even animal spirits are considered egun if honored, specifically in rites and ceremonies called toque de egun. Mentioned in chapter 6.

Egungun - evil ancestral spirits who should be avoided as they can hurt and kill people. Mentioned in chapter 10.

Elegba - known as Legba, elegba are the gatekeepers of the world. They safeguard the doorways between this world and the divine and spiritual realms. Elegba is derived from the name Eleggua (called St. Peter or St. Anthony), a powerful being who guards the crossroads all souls pass after departing. Mentioned in chapters 4 and 5.

Eyo festival - known as the Adamu Orisha Play. This festival is traditionally held to escort the spirit of a deceased king or chief and help welcome his successor. Mentioned in chapter 10.

Fet Gede - known as "Festival day of the dead," is a celebration in Haitian Voodoo. Mentioned in chapters 6 and 10.

Fête du Vodoun - a traditional Vodun festival where people dress up as evil spirits and guardians. Mentioned in chapter 10.

Ghede Lwa is one of the most significant Lwa families from West Africa. Mentioned in chapter 4.

Gris-gris - pronounced as "gree-gree," is an act of creating a powerful magical charm. Its creation typically requires combining white and black magic, and due to this, it is only recommended for experienced practitioners. Mentioned in chapter 9.

Haitian Voodoo - Similar to other African religions, Haitian Voodoo is a spiritual practice where the rituals involve foods, drinks, and herbs for healing and spiritual purposes. Mentioned in chapter 1.

Hoodoo - pronounced as "who-doo," is a magical practice incorporating folk traditions and herbal medicine. It also involves conjuring and other magical practices related to the similarly named Voodoo. Hoodoo combines African spiritual practice with European and Native American beliefs. Mentioned in chapter 1.

Ifa - the central dogma in the Yoruba religion. Mentioned in chapter 1.

Igogo festival - a celebration of the Orisha Oronsen and the yam harvest. Mentioned chapter 10.

Isfet - means disorder and stands in deep contrast to maat, which was created to abolish isfet. Mentioned in chapter 2.

Juju - pronounced as "joo-joo," is a Voodoo term for charms used for protection, healing, and other positive magical purposes.

Ka - this refers to one of the most fundamental parts of the soul as described in Kemetic traditions. Mentioned in chapter 2.

Kemetic Orthodoxy - an ancient Egyptian belief system, according to which the creators made the souls, and the deities guided them. Mentioned in chapter 1.

Lwa - known as loa, a lwa is a powerful spirit who, according to certain African spiritual traditions, governs the different realms of the natural world and can be asked for help, like saints and the Orishas in other religions. Mentioned in chapters 1 and 4.

Ma'at - also called Maat, signifies truth, order, justice, or balance. It represents a fundamental dogma in Kemetic beliefs and is linked to the deity of the same name. Mentioned in chapter 2.

Manman - a term of high respect used for female Lwas. It means mother and has the same bearing for the living elders. Mentioned in chapter 4.

Mojo - a Voodoo term used for charms to bring specific benefits, such as financial, protective, emotional, etc. Mentioned in chapter 9.

Mojo bag - for powerful spells, Voodoo practitioners use small bags filled with crystals, animal parts like fur, bones, feathers, and dried plants. These are called mojo bags and are used to harness or ward off the power. Mentioned in chapter 9.

Netjer - a Kemetic term for the source of divine forces. It is believed that all deities originate from Netjer. Mentioned in chapter 1

Olodumare - the Supreme Being and the creator of the universe according to the Yoruba religion. It's a being that only communicates with Orisha and can't be called on by people. Mentioned in chapters 1 and 3.

Opa egun - a thick, straight, and tall wooden branch. It's used to invoke Orishas. Mentioned in chapter 8.

Opet Festival - was one of the most prominent ancient Kemetic holidays. The festival celebrated the deities Amun, Mut, and Khonsu. Mentioned in chapter 10.

Oshun - the Orisha of the rivers, fertility, love, and marriage. Associated with Our Lady of Charity which is an aspect of the Virgin Mary. Mentioned in chapters 4 and 5.

Orisha - in Yoruba beliefs, the Orisha are spiritual beings that oversee other living creatures. They possess powers people can harness for success, spiritual growth, rites of passage, emotional and physical healing, divination, and more. The Orisha answer to the Supreme Being. Mentioned in chapter 1.

Orunmila or Ornula - is the Orisha of wisdom, knowledge, and divination. He is associated with St. Joseph, St. Philip, and St. Francis of Assisi in Christianity. Mentioned in chapters 4 and 5.

Papa - means father and is used for male Lwas. It denotes respect and honor for these powerful beings. Mentioned in chapter 4.

Petro Lwa - is one of the most significant Lwa families, originating from West Africa. Mentioned in chapter 4.

Polytheism - refers to the beliefs that acknowledge more than one deity (often a large number), as is the case in many African spiritual practices. Mentioned in chapter 1.

Ra - the sun god and the creator of the universe according to certain African religions. It's believed that Maat was made out of him. Mentioned in chapter 2.

Rada Lwa - one of the most significant Lwa families, originating from West Africa. Mentioned in chapter 4.

Rootworkers - a popular term for Hoodoo practitioners who use their wisdom to help others in different aspects of life. Mentioned in chapter 1.

Santeria - known as Lucumi in modern times, is a unique religion that incorporates African spiritual practice elements and Christian beliefs. Mentioned in chapters 1 and 5.

Sed festival - known as the Feast of the Tail, Sed is an ancient Kemetic festival commemorating the pharaoh's rule. More specifically, it honors Horus the Younger, the king of the living. Mentioned in chapter 10.

The Field of Reeds - the ancient Egyptians' equivalent to heaven. Mentioned in chapter 2.

The Weighing of the Hearts - is a trial and judgment every person must go through to determine where they would spend their afterlife depending on the life they've led. Mentioned in chapter 2.

Veve - symbols traced during rituals made for invoking and celebrating Lwas. Mentioned in chapter 4.

Voodoo - a magical practice combining rituals in Christian religious acts and African spirituality. Mentioned in chapter 4.

Wag Festival - a celebration commemorating the god Osiris, Mentioned in chapter 10.

Wep Ronpet - the Kemetic New Year, preceded by the 5 Epagomenal Days celebrating the birthdays of the children of Geb and Nut. Mentioned in chapter 10.

Yemaya - the protector of women and the Orisha of seas, mystery, and lakes. She resembles Our Lady of Regala. Mentioned in chapter 4.

Zangbeto - traditional Voodoo guardians that ward off evil influences. Mentioned in chapter 10.

Here's another book by Mari Silva that you might like

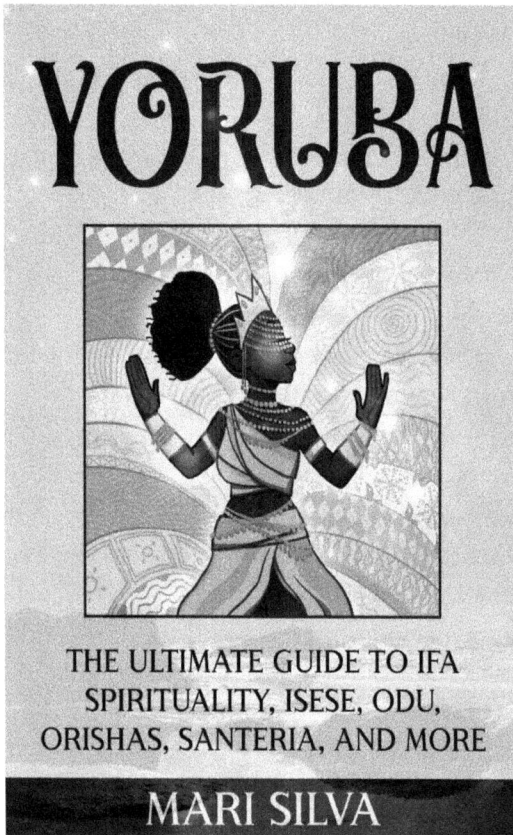

YORUBA

THE ULTIMATE GUIDE TO IFA SPIRITUALITY, ISESE, ODU, ORISHAS, SANTERIA, AND MORE

MARI SILVA

Your Free Gift
(only available for a limited time)

Thanks for getting this book! If you want to learn more about various spirituality topics, then join Mari Silva's community and get a free guided meditation MP3 for awakening your third eye. This guided meditation mp3 is designed to open and strengthen ones third eye so you can experience a higher state of consciousness. Simply visit the link below the image to get started.

https://spiritualityspot.com/meditation

References

Hoodoo in st. Louis: An African American religious tradition (U.s. national Park service). (n.d.). Nps.gov. https://www.nps.gov/articles/000/hoodoo-in-st-louis-an-african-american-religious-tradition.htm

Louissaint, G. (2019, August 21). What is Haitian Voodoo? The Conversation. https://theconversation.com/amp/what-is-haitian-voodoo-119621

The kemetic orthodox religion. (n.d.). Kemet.org. https://www.kemet.org/

The Santeria religion a story. (2009, September 8). African American Registry. https://aaregistry.org/story/from-africa-to-the-americas-santeria/

Wigington, P. (2019, November 29). Yoruba religion: History and beliefs. Learn Religions. https://www.learnreligions.com/yoruba-religion-4777660

42 laws of Maat under Kemet law. (n.d.). Blackhistoryheroes.com. http://www.blackhistoryheroes.com/2013/02/42-laws-of-maat-under-kemet-law-and.html

Ask-Aladdin. (n.d.). Ma'at Egyptian god - Ma'at the god of justice - AskAladdin. Egypt Travel Experts. https://ask-aladdin.com/egypt-gods/maat/

Cressman, D. (2021, October 5). A brief guide to the 7 principles of ma'at - Daniella Cressman. Medium. https://daniellacressman.medium.com/a-brief-guide-to-the-7-principles-of-maat-8ed2faf0fe7c

Elliott, J. (2010, January 1). 3 ways to go on a spiritual journey. WikiHow. https://www.wikihow.com/Go-on-a-Spiritual-Journey

Emily. (2021, October 10). What happens on a spiritual journey? 5 stages you'll experience. Aglow Lifestyle. https://aglowlifestyle.com/what-happens-on-a-spiritual-journey/

Ganguly, I. (2019, October 31). Spiritual journey - complete guide. TheMindFool - Perfect Medium for Self-Development & Mental Health. Explorer of Lifestyle

Abisoye. (2021, August 11). Olodumare, the god with no images, shrines. Plus, TV Africa. https://plustvafrica.com/olodumare-the-god-with-no-images-shrines/

Beyer, C. (2010, February 20). Bondye, the good god of vodou. Learn Religions. https://www.learnreligions.com/bondye-the-good-god-of-vodou-95932

Olódùmarè and the concept of god of the Yoruba people. (2020, March 25). Métissage Sangue Misto. https://metissagesanguemisto.com/olodumare-and-the-concept-of-god-of-the-yoruba-people/

Barrett, O. (2022, February 4). Spirits born out of blood: The lwa of the voodoo pantheon. TheCollector. https://www.thecollector.com/voodoo-lwa/

Beyer, C. (2009, June 4). Vodou Spirits. Learn Religions. https://www.learnreligions.com/spirits-in-african-diaspora-religions-95926

Beyer, C. (2010, February 1). An introduction to the basic beliefs of the vodou (Voodoo) religion. Learn Religions. https://www.learnreligions.com/vodou-an-introduction-for-beginners-95712

Beyer, C. (2012a, June 11). The Orishas. Learn Religions. https://www.learnreligions.com/who-are-the-orishas-95922

Beyer, C. (2012b, June 14). The Orishas: Orunla, Osain, Oshun, Oya, and Yemaya. Learn Religions. https://www.learnreligions.com/orunla-osain-oshun-oya-and-yemaya-95923

demo demo. (2016, September 20). Who are the Orishas? DJONIBA Dance Center. https://www.djoniba.com/who-are-the-orishas/

Gardner, L. (2009, September 29). Cult of the Saints: An Introduction to Santeria. Llewellyn Worldwide. https://www.llewellyn.com/journal/article/2048

"Santeria": La Regla de Ocha-Ifa and Lukumi. (n.d.). Pluralism.Org. https://pluralism.org/%E2%80%9Csanter%C3%ADa%E2%80%9D-the-lucumi-way

Emancipation: The Caribbean Experience. (n.d.). Miami.Edu. https://scholar.library.miami.edu/emancipation/religion1.htm

Regla De Ocha, Candomble, Lucumi, Oyo, Palo, Palo, M., Santeria, M., & Ifa, Y.(n.d.). Orisha Worshippers. Bop.Gov. Retrieved February 10, 2022, from https://www.bop.gov/foia/docs/orishamanual.pdf

mythictreasures. (2020, May 10). Introduction to 7-day candles. Mythictreasures. https://www.mythictreasures.com/post/into-to-7-day-candles

How to invoke the energy of yorube goddess Oshun. (n.d.). Vice.Com. https://www.vice.com/en/article/3kjepv/how-to-invoke-oshun-yoruba-goddess-orisha

admin. (2020, February 1). Fèt Gede - the Haitian Day of the Dead · Visit Haiti. Visit Haiti. https://visithaiti.com/festivals-events/fet-gede-haitian-day-of-the-dead/#:~:text=Every%20year%2C%20on%20November%201

Egun / The ancestors - The Yoruba Religious Concepts. (n.d.). Sites.google.com. https://sites.google.com/site/theyorubareligiousconcepts/egungun-the-ancestors

Herukhuti, R. A. (2022, January 27). Why Africans Honor Ancestral Spirits. https://www.afrikaiswoke.com/the-true-nature-of-african-ancestral-spirits/

Ost, B. (n.d.). LibGuides: African Traditional Religions Textbook: Ifa: Chapter 5. Our Ancestors Are With Us Now. Research.auctr.edu. https://research.auctr.edu/Ifa/Chap5Intro

Voodoo devotees eat GLASS and sacrifice goats during bizarre celebrations held to mark Haiti's day of the dead. (2016, November 2). The Sun. https://www.thesun.co.uk/news/2101053/voodoo-devotees-eat-glass-and-sacrifice-goats-during-bizarre-celebrations-held-to-mark-haitis-day-of-the-dead/

What is Santeria ? - The Yoruba Religious Concepts. (n.d.). Sites.google.com. https://sites.google.com/site/theyorubareligiousconcepts/what-is-santeria

Herb Magic Catalogue: Sampson Snake Root. (n.d.). Www.herbmagic.com. https://www.herbmagic.com/sampson-snake-root.html

High John the Conqueror Root: A Staple of Hoodoo Magic. (n.d.). Original Botanica. Retrieved November 17, 2022, from https://originalbotanica.com/blog/high-john-the-conqueror-root-a-staple-of-hoodoo-magic/ (This website was my main resource for this chapter)

Jimson Weed: History, Perceptions, Traditional Uses, and Potential Therapeutic Benefits of the Genus Datura - American Botanical Council. (n.d.). Www.herbalgram.org. https://www.herbalgram.org/resources/herbalgram/issues/69/table-of-contents/article2930/

SAW PALMETTO. (n.d.). Star Child. https://starchild.co.uk/products/saw-palmetto?variant=12527087550535

Altars of the Yoruba religion. (n.d.). Excelencias.com. https://caribeinsider.excelencias.com/index.php/en/news/altars-yoruba-religion

Dorsey, L. (2014, March 23). Creating ancestor Altars in Santeria, vodou, and voodoo. Voodoo Universe. https://www.patheos.com/blogs/voodoouniverse/2014/03/creating-ancestor-altars-in-santeria-vodou-and-voodoo/

Helena. (2021, January 24). How to build an altar at home for spiritual self-care. Disorient. https://disorient.co/build-an-altar/

LibGuides: African traditional religions textbook: Ifa: Chapter 5. Our ancestors are with us now. (2021). https://research.auctr.edu/Ifa/Chap5Intro

Bradley, J., & Coen, C. D. (2010). Magic's in the bag: Creating spellbinding Gris Gris bags and sachets. Llewellyn Publications.

Caro, T. (2020, September 14). Mojo Bag vs Gris-Gris [the difference & how to use them]. Magickal Spot. https://magickalspot.com/mojo-bag-vs-gris-gris/

How to make your own mojo bags. (n.d.). Nui Cobalt Designs. https://nuicobaltdesigns.com/blogs/daily-astrology-reports/16564821-how-to-make-your-own-mojo-bags

How to: What is a mojo bag and how do I use it? (n.d.). Livejournal.com. https://ldygry.livejournal.com/4248.html

Chery, D. N. (2016, July 29th). AP PHOTOS: Voodoo festival transforms Haitian village. Associated Press.

Feast of the Beautiful Valley. (2021, May 1st). Kemetic Temple UK. https://kemetictemple.uk/t/feast-of-the-beautiful-valley/618

Festival of the wag. (n.d.). Historyofegypt.net. https://historyofegypt.net/?page_id=980

Festivals. (n.d.). Kemet.org. https://www.kemet.org/community/festivals